Praise for Maui CEO: Import from China, Sell on eBay, and Live Wherever You Want

"My Dad is starting an eBay business based on *Maui CEO!*" Matt Carey, CTO and VP, eBay

"Unlike today's hot book—*The 4-hour Workweek*—John has penned a framework that makes fighting the big-guys possible and practical. *Maui CEO* is the ultimate expression of buying low and using e-commerce to leverage a small business." Dean Gualco, PhD., Professor of e-commerce at four universities

"John understands the marketplace and is able to ask the tough questions, set the boundaries, and connect the dots—even if the answer is contrary to popular opinion." Elie Ofek, Associate Professor of Business, Harvard Business School

"John's approach is the perfect blend of applying academic frameworks in a practical way." Paul Carlile, Associate Professor, Boston University

"Maui CEO gives point-blank advice on how to make your trip to China, and dealings with Chinese manufacturers, successful. I love it. Clear, concise, and actionable. Use it and prosper." James Kyle, Chief of Staff to Chinese executive and resident of Beijing, China.

"I've made my first trip to China and Maui CEO has helped me every step of the way." Robert Johnson, Synergy Exchange Solutions

"John Tennant is the most talented and practical executive I have ever worked with. He was born to lead others." Susan McCabe, former VP of Sales, Avon, and VP of Business Development, Xerox

The Maui CEO

The Maui CEO

✦

**Import from China, Sell on eBay, and
Live Wherever You Want**

John Tennant

iUniverse, Inc.
New York Lincoln Shanghai

The Maui CEO
Import from China, Sell on eBay, and Live Wherever You Want

iUniverse books may be ordered through booksellers or by contacting:

iUniverse
2021 Pine Lake Road, Suite 100
Lincoln, NE 68512
www.iuniverse.com
1-800-Authors (1-800-288-4677)

Because of the dynamic nature of the Internet, any Web addresses or links contained in this book may have changed since publication and may no longer be valid.

ISBN: 978-0-595-34032-3 (pbk)
ISBN: 978-0-595-78820-0 (ebk)

Printed in the United States of America

For Terri,

Who means everything to me,

And for my kids,

May you learn from my mistakes and efforts and be better than I ever was.

Contents

Introduction

Cleveland. El Paso. Atlanta. What is the common thread? Each city is full of people who don't want to live there. These people have taken job opportunities based on the employer's location and the job offer—but not necessarily on what the location has to offer the employee individually.

Put another way, would you rather live in Cleveland or Maui? Most would answer Maui, based on the island's good weather, and the image of excellent mental and physical health. Maui is of course only representative of any ideal location; living in the mountains of Switzerland may be equally appealing. Regardless of this ideal location's name, the reason you don't live there is likely because you can't find a good job in Maui. Selling timeshares isn't what you had in mind, right?

Maui CEO shows you how to start your own business, specifically designed from the ground up to managed remotely from anywhere you want. One of the biggest challenges to a new business is building systems and structures without a clear framework. Maui CEO solves this challenge. This book is your blueprint, and will show you how to select a product; buy that product in China; import the goods into the U.S.; and sell and deliver online, particularly through eBay.

This second edition deepens the content from the first edition, and utilizes feedback received from readers like you via email. One thing I haven't changed is the size of the book. I was in a bus in Taiwan and saw a guy reading Maui CEO; when I asked him about it, the first thing he identified was how convenient the book was to physically carry around with him and make notes as he thought about each section. While this book may be shorter than others you are considering, Maui CEO is heavy on content. I don't waste a lot of space on fluff—the shorter the book, the smaller the environmental impact ... and your chances for success are increased as the book's length tightens your focus.

The original concept was to have two separate books, the first book addressing pre-launch activities and the other tackling post-launch growth. In retrospect, customers wanted everything in one concise place. Finally, a lot of changed since the first edition was published in 2005. Skype went from practically nothing to having over 200M users and being a viable part of your telco strategy, for instance. To make sure you're getting the latest and greatest, I've taken executive education courses on Marketing and Strategy at Harvard and MIT this year, and have attended (and spoke at) eBay Live and the eBay Developer's Conferences in 2006 and 2007.

I believe your chances for future success are high because Maui CEO is practical.

This guide is practical for two reasons: first, you are provided detailed content. I provide you specific information rather than broad platitudes. For instance, instead of advising you to "go incorporate," I explain why; tell you specifically to incorporate in Nevada; and give you the name, number, and URL of the best place to help you incorporate. Second, this guide is practical because I am also your project manager. I provide you a "project plan" which gives you the right order of milestones and tasks. This way, you can reduce redundancy and get your business up and running as fast as possible. I would venture a guess that this book will give you a 9 month advantage minimum over someone else trying to figure all of this out on their own.

Why am I qualified to write this book? Because I have done everything I will be asking you to do, and have the benefit of successes and failures to draw upon. In the small business world, I have started California and Nevada corporations; created a dot-com which lead its field (until a divorce gutted the capital base); and managed or outsourced every type of small business function, from advertising to accounting. In the large business world, I have worked for such well-known companies as Intel, Hewlett-Packard, Domino's Pizza International, and WordPerfect. I also hold a J.D. and MBA from the University of Michigan, and have taught graduate-level E-commerce and business strategy courses at the University of Phoenix. My knowledge and experience are current, and you are the beneficiary.

Now, on to some assumptions: first, I am writing this book not to the academic establishment, but instead to the person who has always dreamed of being an entrepreneur. This category of reader could realistically include a corporate-type who wants to spend more time with his or her children; a spouse who is bored of the tennis scene; a displaced Southern Californian who longs to return to the beach; or a Starbucks manager.

A manager at Starbucks is actually the ideal candidate to start an online global business. This person, while neither a Harvard MBA nor a frequent target of Korn Ferry headhunters, has the "smarts," exposure to good processes, and $22,000 (or so) it will take to get things going.

I also assume that you've already decided to start your business. You've read the latest books and articles, such as Michael Gerber's[1] text on why most small businesses don't work. In other words, the scope of this book does not address whether you have what it takes to be successful. I will give you a valuable head start—the rest is up to you.

Another important assumption is that no venture capitalist will want to invest in this business you will be creating. Based on my experience at venture capital conferences, you can expect venture equity investment only if you can reasonably grow your business to from $0 to $50M in revenue—in three years. We all have dreams of starting a cool company, only to be bought by Yahoo or Google. I too had this vision, but now I know better. You should instead plan your business with one of these two exit strategies in mind: 1) either sell your successful business to a larger entity after 4 or 5 years; or 2) move to Hawaii and run your business from there. In the latter scenario, you <u>don't</u> exit the business but manage it in your mornings and play island golf in the afternoons. You become the Maui CEO!

A final assumption is that you are initially targeting American consumers. North Americans have the money and market size to deserve your focus. After establishing the success of your business, you can eventually expand globally.

Moving on, a common focus on eBay runs through both the texts. eBay is your most important channel—at least for now—and therefore dominates thematically. Ebay is organized by category, and our joint goal is to dominate that competitive group. I will show you how to create an eBay category killer.

---

1.   Michael Gerber, *The E-Myth Revisited: Why Most Small Businesses Don't Work and What to Do About It*, (HarperBusiness 1995).

1

Setting Your Core Business Strategy

There are three possible core business strategies, and I highlight why you should be a low-cost leader.

In the Fall of 2004, I bought a business suit on eBay. The suit, made by Italy's Ermenegildo Zegna, legitimately retails at my local (and fancy) men's store for $1495. That's right—$1500 (plus $116 in tax)! My eBay price? Including shipping and insurance, $309. This instance illustrates a few key points:

1. EBay, which will undoubtedly be one of your sales channels, is really setting the market price at the wholesale, not retail, level. Sure, we've all heard the stories of someone buying a Barbie doll for $20 and selling the doll on eBay for $600. These "feel good" stories do not apply to you and your new business. You will be competing with other businesses at the wholesale—and lower—price levels.

2. Therefore, you need to be able to buy product below whole-sale—much, much lower. You accomplish this by purchasing bulk goods from China or another low-cost source. More information on buying by the container load will be provided later in chapters 5 and 6.

3. I bought the suit online because of its low price. I would **not** have bought this item online if the price were close or equal to the local retail price.

This final illustration is important: the customer won't risk their money on a large purchase unless the savings are significant from the off-line, traditional "store." The amount of difference is subject to debate because many times it is an emotional decision, and also includes many variables such as shipping timeframe.

Consider the following scenario: you are looking at a fancy Viking stainless steel refrigerator. It costs $4200 at your local, high-end kitchen appliance store. How much would you pay if you bought it online? Here's a good summary of how each channel would relate to each other:

Channel	How Much You Would Pay (Relative)		
Local high-end store:	Highest		
Nice, crisp website which sells only refrigerators:	Medium		
Crappy website selling lots of appliances:	Lowest (approximate tie)		
eBay:	Lowest (approximate tie)		

Here are some conclusions I've drawn with my experience in this area:

- If buying online, you would pay a little bit more from a website that looked professional; loaded fast and was clearly navigable. This is no surprise. A 'crappy' website tends to connotate that the product quality—and definitely the service—is and will be somehow less.

- The price you would pay from the nice, crisp website is (sometimes slightly) higher than eBay. Why? eBay as a channel has commoditized the buyers and products (but not sellers). Buyers want and usually get low prices on eBay, and it's easy for buyers to sort by price, compare products and model numbers, and buy low. Also, the generic worry about "fraud" on eBay pushes down the Average Selling Prices (ASPs) across the board. Unless a specific website or company has gotten bad press about fraud (like TJ Maxx), you worry just a little bit less. For instance, if I buy that refrigerator on eBay, I have to worry about a) the seller, b) eBay itself, and c) PayPal. Something can go wrong in either of those three areas, or so I think. In contrast, if I buy from 'Crazy Eddy's Viking Refrigerators' online, I really only have to worry about Crazy Eddie's employee capturing my credit card number. In short, buyers will pay a little more from a nice online store than buying the same item on eBay.

- You would pay a little bit more at your local retailer. But not much! Again, this is a function of many variables, like whether the item is in stock; warranty and return policies; how much extra you have to pay in taxes; the availability of financing; and so on.

As you consider your own conclusions here, translate those conclusions into a definition of your own biases.

Selecting Your Core Business Identity

Let me take a step back, for the moment, and describe a key concept from the off-line world that really sets your core business strategy. Put forth in detail by the wonderful book *Discipline of Market Leaders,*[2] the authors' argument is that you must be either a

- Product Leader (Ferrari, Intel, and Rolex);
- Total Solution Provider (Saks Fifth Avenue and Xerox); or
- Low-Cost Leader (Wal-Mart, Fry's, and Dollar Tree).

The idea is simple: examination of market leaders lead the author to conclude that each company listed above was successful because they were extremely good at focusing and executing on one of the three values. Ferrari cars are typically faster and cooler than anything else; Saks has people that remember your name, computers that remember your preferences, and a nice culture of ass-kissing; and at Dollar Tree, everything is, well, a dollar. These are good brick-and-mortar examples of product, solution, and low-cost leaders.

---

2.   Michael Traecy and Fred Wiersma, *The Discipline of Market Leaders: Choose Your Customers, Narrow Your Focus, Dominate Your Market,* (Perseus Books Group, 1997).

Who are the online-only leaders of today? Who do you hear most about? Here are a few:

- Product Leader (Google, MySpace, CNN);
- Total Solution Provider (Amazon, CNET); or
- Low-Cost Leader (?).

The lack of a "house-hold" name in low-cost leadership (online only) does not mean that they don't exist; rather, low-cost is a horizontal value proposition across most online-only businesses, and therefore don't get the press that other leaders have. For instance, Skype sells telephone minutes that cost less than half of what the incumbent telephone carriers charge; carried 4.4% of all international telephone calls last year[3]; is not re-branded and re-sold by other companies; and yet, has less than 5% brand recognition in the U.S, according to Interbrand[4]. My previous "dot-com" shipped 450 pound objects to 46 states, Mexico, Canada, Aruba, Belgium, and Poland. We had $600,000 in sales the second year and $1M the third year, and yet the established offline leader had not even heard of us. Online-only low-cost leaders do exist, and you're going to be one of them.

If you're still not convinced, consider the latest available eBay Buyer Segmentation Study from June 2006[5]. eBay themselves segment as follows:

- Shopping Driven Passionate
- Convenience Driven Enthusiast
- Value-Driven (Low Price)
- Bargain Seekers (Low Price)

---

3.   Telegeography survey December 1 2006. See http://www.telegeography.com/cu/article.php?article_id=15656
4.   http://www.brandchannel.com/boty_results/us_2005.html
5.   "Lessons from eBay Buyer Research," Jeff Resnick of eBay, at the 2007 eBay Developer's Conference (Boston)

As eBay looked at each segment's spending patterns in their "Share of Wallet Tracking" research[6], eBay concluded that the latter two segments shop online 160M times per month; buy around 60M items per month; and shop twice as often as the other two segments. Finally, eBay's "Top Buyer Lapse/Decline" June 2006 research[7] found out that "the deals [on eBay] just don't seem to be as good as they used to be." eBay as a marketplace has commoditized many of the products; you have a better way, however. Let's move on.

Going back to the *Discipline of Market Leaders* for a moment: the book points out that these category leaders develop and focus on their value proposition, while only being mediocre in the other values! These are my words, not theirs, but I love the concept. Not paying heed to this principle is a big reason why online low-cost leaders fail.

For illustration, Rolex is an effective product leader because the customer believes that if they buy a Rolex, they are getting the world's best quality watch.[8] When buying from a product leader, the customer *does not expect* low prices from the dealer. In fact, low prices would weaken the product leader image that I am expecting when I "hire"[9] the product. Finding low prices at the Maui Ritz-Carlton, on a Tiffany ring, or on a new Mercedes actually goes against your (the buyer's) expectations. Similarly, when a customer shops at Wal-Mart or Fry's, that customer is primarily expecting low prices. They do not expect Nordstrom service or E. Zegna suits.

---

6.   Quoted and referenced in "Lessons from eBay Buyer Research," Jeff Resnick of eBay, at the 2007 eBay Developer's Conference (Boston)

7.   Quoted and referenced in "Lessons from eBay Buyer Research," Jeff Resnick of eBay, at the 2007 eBay Developer's Conference (Boston)

8.   Interestingly, Rolex is considered by experts to be inferior in product quality to the products of a dozen other manufacturers. Similarly, Steinway is not considered by experts to be the best-made or sounding piano, nor is Volvo considered to be the safest automobile. However, all three companies have successfully branded their products so that images of heavy watches, concert pianos, and safe cars "pop" into our minds in relationship to those brands.

9.   Clayton M. Christensen and Michael E. Raynor, *The Innovator's Solution: Creating and Sustaining Successful Growth* (Harvard Business School Press, 2003).

Therefore, when you select your core business "discipline," you *must* focus on providing that discipline and that value alone. If customers are not expecting Nordstrom service, then you should neither fund nor provide Nordstrom service.

If it is not obvious yet, let me say that I believe that you should be a low-cost leader. Here's why:

You do not have the resources to be a product leader, at least at this point. In the structure I outline in the following chapters, you cannot make or buy camcorders better than Sony. Also, legitimate multinational companies who **are** product leaders will not likely sell you product—just so that you can turn around and sell online right into their dealer territories. Being a product leader does not mean having a wide and deep product line offering. In fact, this is a bad idea primarily because it is not competitively defensible. For illustration, if you decide to focus on technical computer books and touted your "wide selection as a product leader," the current category leader can always match and beat your product line depth by offering more selections than you can.

Because of economies of scale, resources, and dealer agreements, you cannot be a product leader online. What about the second value proposition, namely being a total solution provider?

Xerox is an effective total solution provider because Xerox Business Solutions knows your business better than you do. To prove their point, Xerox has recently agreed to come in and manage your entire printer, copier, scanner, and fax machine fleet—and will do so at 80% of your cost[10]. Your yearly costs (toner, paper, maintenance, network drops, and so on) are agreed upon. If you spend $5M a year on these items, then Xerox will agree to take over the whole ball of wax for $4M. How can they do this

---

10.   Based on several conversations between me and Xerox employees.

and still make a profit? Because Xerox understands "managed document services," end to end, better than you do.

Here's the issue regarding you and your new business: You can't provide the appropriate levels of warranty and repair service remotely. If you sell Jacuzzis, for instance, how are you supposed to fix the heater or repair the cracked fiberglass—in all 50 States—from your hammock in Maui? Additionally, for reasons that will be evident soon, you will be selling a product, not a service. "Product solutions" are sold more effectively by a local, off-line presence. *Maui CEO* does not speak to service-based businesses; I believe successful online service businesses will either be based on product leader reputation (like Johnny Cochran offering legal services), a new category that can thrive and be a killer app (such as 'career coaching'), or being the exchange itself that all other service businesses integrate with, through, and/or on top of. Low cost is not sustainable in the services businesses, at least at this time. For instance, using videocams, why can't you help students with their math skills from Maui? Because someone in India, Malaysia, or Russia will do it cheaper.

The remaining strategic option for product-based businesses is, of course, low-cost leader. As opposed to the services space described above, low-cost leadership works for our purposes in the product space. Customers buying online expect a good deal, and you have designed your organization from the ground up to deliver. A successful low-cost leader does not sponsor the local polo match or have a marble lobby, and they do not over-invest in presentation and service. They are disciplined about low-cost leadership.

You have just completed the first step in your business plan. Our mission is to be a low-cost leader. Low-cost leader in what? you might ask. We're going to decide what kind of product to sell in the next chapter.

2

Deciding Which Product to Buy for Resale

Worried that you and 50 others will be selling the same thing on eBay? Seek barriers to entry. I give clear guidelines on product branding, quality, and targeting businesses versus individual consumers.

Selling the Same Thing on eBay?

You should be worried. On a product as specific as the suit I mentioned in last chapter, there are at one moment in time 188 E. Zegna suits for sale by at least 22 different sellers.[11] As I mentioned earlier, eBay will almost certainly be one of your sales channels. You can't ignore eBay's contribution to your Total Available Market. According to an April 2007 press release, eBay has 233 million registered and about 100 million active users.[12] Importantly, the number of registered users continues to grow at a healthy clip.[13]

Consider this consumer electronics example: For something as "exclusive" as a plasma television, the phrase "plasma tv" returned 1014 items for sale![14]

---

11.   Search performed Thursday, October 7, 2004, at 3:40 p.m. PST.
12.   Q1'2007 Financial results available on www.ebay.com.
13.   "Confirmed Registered Users—Cumulative confirmed registered users at the end of Q1-04 totaled a record 104.8 million, representing a 52% increase over the 68.8 million users reported at the end of Q1-03." 2007 results available on www.ebay.com.

The Internet tends to commoditize products. For us, this means that product differentiation is difficult to achieve. Recent data implies that 49% of Internet shoppers are making their purchase decisions based on **price alone.**[15] What can you do?

Seek Barriers to Entry

Classic Marketing theory suggests two options: (a) Make customer switching costs high; and (b) look for or create barriers to entry. Switching costs tie customers into your product or service. Cell phone companies used to make customer switching costs high with number portability. In other words, the companies made it difficult for you to switch carriers because you could not take your phone number with you from one carrier (i.e., Verizon) to the next carrier (i.e., AT&T). It took a recent FCC ruling[16] to remove the number portability barrier. Cell phone companies then re-priced handsets so that customers sign one or two-year contracts in order to have the handset subsidized. If the Apple iPhone successfully gets AT&T new customers from other carriers despite the barriers, well, the carriers will seek additional ways to make switching costs high!

This is wonderful for the businesses that can make switching costs high for their customers. If you decided to follow a Business-to-Business model, you can explore ways to impose high switching costs on your customers. For instance, you could seek a 3-year contract with a significant cancellation penalty as a way of penalizing a switch from you to someone else. I bring this up as a reminder that as a way to crate barriers to entry by competitors, ideally your product or service is "sticky" and switching to a competitor is not easy or cheap.

14. Search performed Saturday, June 30, 2007, at 3:44 p.m. PST.
15. Rayport and Jaworkski (2004). *Introduction to eCommerce (2nd ed.)*. New York: McGraw-Hill, pg 114.
16. Action by the Commission, November 7, 2003, by Memorandum Opinion and Order and Further Notice of Proposed Rulemaking (FCC 03-284). See http://www.fcc.gov/cgb/NumberPortability.

Here is the book's first shocker: in our model, you won't have many repeat customers, and therefore no need to create high switching costs. In today's online product world, buyers frequently "Google" the product; read the reviews and blogs and specs; and buy from the cheapest site that looks reputable and safe. In many consumer purchases under $100, the buyer can't even tell you the name of the site they used 24 hours later. All of these factors—namely 0% unaided brand awareness, half of all buyers purchasing on price alone—mean that you should not try to create high switching costs.

That said, you will probably not be able to make switching costs high in an online product business. As I will explore shortly, it is likely you will be selling large, expensive items such as pool tables, pianos, or Jacuzzis. If your model targets customers (and not businesses), you won't have many repeat customers[17] anyway—hence no need to seek high switching costs.

In contrast to high switching costs, you can and *must* look for barriers to entry. A classic barrier to entry is something that deters others from competing against you.[18] For instance, let's say you decide you want to turn your hobby of building cool cars into a business like De Lorean.[19] The challenge of competing successfully against Porsche and Toyota is monumental, given the costs of designing and producing just one of your new cars. The barriers that exist from your perspective eventually keep you out of the market. These barriers include the obvious industry characteristics like a large number of competitors, frequent price wars (with 0% financing), and the relative inflexibility of the distribution system. In other words, why would car dealers sell your new car? Other barriers keeping

---

17.   I am well aware of the argument that customer bonding and repeat business both create barriers to entry and high switching costs. See *The Delta Project: Discovering New Sources of Profitability in a Networked Economy*. I don't think this is the right way to look at the problem in our networked economy.

18.   M.E. Porter, "How Competitive Forces Shape Strategy," *Harvard Business Review*, March—April 1979, pp. 137-45.

19.   See http://www.delorean.com/

you at bay inevitably come down to the disparity in cost positions—you can match neither GM's economies of scale nor their experience curve.[20]

Not to worry. In the product world, in OUR world, here is what you do to keep the threat of new entrants reduced:

- **Buy and sell products that weigh more than 150 lbs**. This is the maximum weight that U.P.S. will deliver. If a product weighs more than 150 lbs, or has unusually large dimensions, the item must be put on a pallet and shipped by a freight company. Examples could include the following:

  - caskets[21]

  - huge pottery

  - Jacuzzis

  - koi ponds

  - decorative rocks

  - large antiques

  - furniture

  - stainless steel kitchen appliances

  - large medical equipment

  - tractors (used or new)

  - wave runners

  - scooters

  - industrial tires

---

20. For an interesting discussion of experience versus learning curves, see generally Pearce and Robinson, "Strategic Management: Formulation, Implementation, and Control of Competitive Strategy," *McGraw-Hill/Irwin*; 8th edition (August 19, 2002).
21. Interestingly enough, it appears that funeral homes are required by law to offer services to all customers, even if a casket is not purchased from the funeral home. See the Federal Trade Commission's "Funeral Rule" 16 CFR Part 453.

- kids outdoor play equipment
- preformed construction equipment
- anything else BIG and/or heavy.

By having a product that can't easily be shipped, you create a barrier that will probably be around for a decade—longer than most barriers and a key aspect of your strategy. I'll explain how to ship large freight and get 50% discounts on freight shipping later.

Buying and selling products that weigh more than 150 lbs is *the* key way to limit competition within your eBay category. This is backed up by data which shows that large, heavy items have much lower sell-through percentages than easy-to-ship (and easy to copy) items. To illustrate, I'll take three products from above and compare them to top sellers on eBay as of June 30, 2007 (data from May 2007).

Item	# for sale	# sold	Sell-through %
Any brand upright piano	127	70	55.1%
Viking refrigerator	39	22	56.4%
John Deere tractors	851	513	60.3%
Happy Feet' DVD	1,082	974	90.0%
Cell phones w/o contracts	2,281	1,387	60.8%
Apple iPod	78,455	54,620	69.6%

A lower sell-through percentage points to difficulty or pricing gaps somewhere in the system; my belief is that the trouble associated with and cost of shipping large items is the key culprit—something you will become very good at (shipping large items, that is). Note also the sheer number of items for sale in the smaller goods means more competition and lower prices for all sellers.

For those of you not sold on this idea, you can utilize XML and technology to create "virtual" inventory and processes which will help you achieve low-cost status: but you will never be a low-cost leader in that space. Other ways to keep the threat of new entrants reduced include:

- **Focus your business around a small product line**. Having 50 items for sale, or 500 or 5 million, is never a sustainable competitive position, because a better-funded competitor can always match and beat your product line size. Most businesses make the majority of profit on a small number of popular products. For instance, the Bluthner Piano Company[22] offers grand pianos in six sizes and countless finishes, including mahogany, flame mahogany, pyramid mahogany, ash, beech, white, cherry, walnut, walnut with burl inlay, jacaranda, jacaranda wood fitted with leather, and ebony. However, according to Bluthner's president, 95% of all grand pianos sold are finished in ebony.[23] Bluthner needs to offer pianos in all of these finishes because they are a product leader—you do not. You would do well to pick one grand piano size—or two sizes at the most—and sell only ebony.

- **Sell your product entirely online** to compete against the big corporation. Most organizations prohibit others, or are prohibited themselves, from selling online. This prohibition—effectively a barrier in your favor—is to protect the established dealer network and to keep some kind of control on prices. I've run lots of calculations on small businesses renting local retail space ... and the additional revenues just don't add up.

- **Buy your product by container-load from China** to compete against other small competitors. I tell you how and why in chapters 5 and 6. I fyou buy from the U.S. distributor, you cannot have a true low-cost advantage and you play by their rules.

- **Establish a PowerSeller[24] rating on eBay** as soon as possible. PowerSellers are top eBay sellers with high sales and positive feedback. According to my observation and experience, eBay PowerSellers can achieve a much higher margin than a one-time or infrequent seller—based on the PowerSeller's reputation and eBay feedback score alone.[25] For instance, Jennie Blaser and Marissa Johnson tracked every piano listed and sold on eBay in March, April and

22. http://www.bluthnerpiano.com/
23. Verbal conversation with Christian Bluthner, January 2004, Anaheim California.
24. http://pages.ebay.com/services/buyandsell/welcome.html

June 2003. In April 2003, 153 pianos were sold. The Average Selling Price ("ASP") of the lone eBay PowerSeller was $6,233, compared to everyone else's ASP of $2,807. In June 2004, the average selling price for upright pianos (by PowerSeller) was $1,867, versus everyone else's ASP of $1,207. eBay is the focus of chapter 10.

- **Learn the ins and outs of Logistics Management** and how to maximize your shipping discounts will also be very important. I show you how later in this book.

Which Product Do You Buy For Resale?

You already know the most important criterion: that the product's shipping weight is too large and/or heavy for U.P.S. to deliver. I have one more suggestion: pick a product that you know almost nothing about. Why? Because one's intimate product knowledge can cloud their early execution and decision-making. As referenced earlier, current authors believe that product experts (or "technicians") make lousy entrepreneurs.[26] By picking a product you know little about, you can make clearer decisions about product branding, selection, and so on. And really, how hard is it to research everything you need to know about pool tables?

I have a new service on mauiceo.com called the eBay Sales Assistant, which will help you analyze a product every which way imaginable.… giving you hard data with which to consider and calculate your future success.

Speaking of pool tables, let's quickly discuss product branding, quality, and segmentation—in the context of pool tables.

25. For instance, Jennie Blaser and Marissa Johnson tracked every piano listed and sold on eBay in March, April, and June 2003. In April 2003, 153 pianos were sold. The Average Selling Price (ASP) of the lone eBay PowerSeller was $ 6,233, compared to everyone else's ASP of $ 2,807. In June 2004, the average selling price for upright pianos (by PowerSeller) was $ 1,867, versus everyone else's ASP of $1,207.
26. Michael E. Gerber. *The E-Myth Revisited: Why Most Small Businesses Don't Work and What to do About It.* HarperBusiness, 2004)

Using Your Own House Brand (Product Branding)

In chapter 3, I discuss the importance of your corporate identity and connection between identity and branding.

At this point in the text, it is important to set your expectations regarding product branding. What name are you going to put on your pool/billiard tables? How about Brunswick? Everyone would like to sell Brunswick pool tables, because Brunswick has a good reputation. However, as you may or may not know, Brunswick will not let you sell their pool tables online. Why? If you sell a pool table to a buyer in Omaha, Nebraska, for instance, the authorized Brunswick dealer just *lost* that local sale. Worse, the buyer probably used your Web price as leverage against the dealer, whose cost structure is higher than yours, forcing the dealer to decide between 15% margin or losing the sale.

Therefore, you use your own "house" brand. A Google search on *pool tables* yielded a Web site selling brands like Showood[27] and Black Bear.[28] When you get a company in China (or anywhere, for that matter) to put your name on their product, this process is called an Original Equipment Manufacturer (OEM) agreement.

The obvious question you might have is why would someone buy a Black Bear billiard table instead of a Brunswick? The answer is price. Here is a surprising and important piece of data: Customers pay only 3.1% more for brand-name items online.[29] This data comes from a study of consumer behavior on a *shop bot*.[30] A shop bot lets consumers compare sellers and

---

27.   Trademarks and brand names are the rights of their respective owners. See http://www.cornerstonebilliards.com/. Search done on Tuesday, October 19, 2004, at 10:21a.m. PST.
28.   Trademarks and brand names are the rights of their respective owners. See http://www.cornerstonebilliards.com/. Search done on Tuesday, October 19, 2004, at 10:21a.m. PST.
29.   Mitch Betts, *"Brands Still Matter, Even for Shopbots,"* MIT "Sloan Management Review" (Winter 2001) pg 9.

prices on a singular product. My longtime favorite has been www.mysimon.com. Once you choose the product (say, a particular digital camera), the "bot" finds Web prices for that model and sorts the data based on the vendor paying the most for this privilege. The output data can then be sorted by low price, including shipping and collected sales tax (if applicable).

This data leads me to a conclusion: Don't over-invest in your brand development. Beyond the initial design of your logo and development of your brand information and positioning (see chapter 3), monies spent on *prod-*

---

30. A *shop bot* lets consumers compare sellers and prices on a singular product. My longtime favorite has been www.mySimon.com. Once you choose the product (say, a particular digital camera), the "bot" finds Web prices for that model and sorts the data based on the vendor paying the most for this privilege. The output data can then be sorted by low price, including shipping and collected sales tax (if applicable).

uct brand development are wasted this early in the business life. In fact, Professor Clayton Christensen of Harvard Business School points out that in certain segments, valuable brands are not on the products but on the channel itself—such as Old Navy or eBay. (*The Innovator's Solution*, page 165.)

Another key reason for using your own house brand—perhaps the most practical—is that you have total control. If you are selling someone else's brand, either legitimately or otherwise, you are subject to that brand owner's heavy hand. A common discussion topic at the 2007 eBay Live conference was how manufacturers are asking volume sellers to avoid eBay or face loss of buying privileges. If you violate a company's selling policies, you loose your ability to buy product from the company or their resellers. Ways companies are combating the sale of their products online include the following:

- **Minimum advertised prices (MAP)**. These mean you cannot list a sale price lower than the company-set floor.

- **Territory**. Companies don't want you to sell, or even quote, outside of your granted "territory."

- **Demo**. To avoid saying a product is "new," companies force sellers to claim phrases such as "demo," "scratch & dent," "warranty does not transfer," and so forth.

- **VeRO program**. This is strong-arm enforcement tactics through eBay.

In my mind, this is one of the biggest changes affecting eBay sellers in the history of eBay.

Avoid Getting Stung by EBay's VeRO Program

EBay's Verified Rights Owner (VeRO) Program[31] was apparently created to help cut back on the sale of counterfeit items. My first observation of counterfeit items for sale on eBay was seeing the New York City fake Rolex watches. Given the sheer volume of auctions, eBay decided to shift responsibility of intellectual property protection to the companies.

Let me illustrate this with a personal, real-life example from Fall 2004. I was visiting my mother in Utah and bought a McIntosh[32] amplifier ($6,000 list) from the local authorized dealer. I decided to sell the product two months later and listed the amp for sale in a Buy It Now auction on eBay. The manufacturer, McIntosh Laboratories/Parasound Products, Inc., had the auction shut down (before the 7-day auction period expired) through VeRO. Just like that. I as the seller was not contacted prior to the auction being shut down,[33] and the auction text is subsequently not available in your Unsold category so that you can see what violated policy, or to aid you in relisting the item appropriately. In other words, it's a big pain!

---

31. See http://pages.ebay.com/help/confidence/vero-removed-listing.html and http://pages.ebay.com/help/community/vero-aboutme.html

32. www.mcintoshlabs.com

33. The process apparently works as follows: the intellectual property holder notifies eBay VeRO of the "violation," eBay visually verifies the claim, then eBay shuts down the auction. The IP holder sends this kind of e-mail to eBay: "Please act expeditiously to remove the following listing. Item no. xxxxxxxxxx, which infringes IP owner's registered U.S. trademarks, including No. y,yyy,yyy, and infringes IP owner's copyrighted materials. This ad has unlawfully reproduced IP owner's copyrighted product photographs, which have been downloaded from IP owner's Web site without IP owner's permission. For confirmation, please go to http://www.zzzzzz.com." The problem is procedural: While the IP holder must specifically identify the offending portion of the auction (i.e., photos or text), eBay does not pass this information on to the seller. The seller is only notified that "your listing uses a rights owner's image and/or copyrighted text without authorization." When I finally got ahold of the law firm (see next note), even they could not provide me proof (i.e., a copy of the auction) of my offense. In the end result, a relatively innocent party does not know exactly what he or she did wrong.

There is currently, in my opinion, no effective appeal process. I sent three e-mails to the address listed, with an inadequate response time.[34]

I believe what violated the owner's intellectual property was my use of a stock photo image from their Web site.[35] So I relisted the item using my own photos. Within 9 days of the auction start, the manufacturer used the serial number (visible in the photos) to figure out who sold me the item. McIntosh then threatened in a retaliatory manner the seller with his dealership rights. So my twenty-year relationship with this small-business owner (and his very livelihood, given the importance of the McIntosh line to his profitability) are challenged by this VeRO program. And I was a valid titleholder to the product!

Take it from me—this time next year, small business owners will not be able to effectively sell new, brand-name products on eBay like today. You must understand this. EBay will be your most effective channel in the early stages of your business life. The small business model of buying used junk at local garage stores, then selling the items on eBay, does not generate enough revenue for you to live on—much less live in Maui. There are hosts of more successful small businesses on eBay today, but they sell Tommy Bahama shirts, Linksys routers, Panasonic televisions, and Swiss Army knives. These items will not be for sale next year by anyone other than authorized resellers, under the thumbs and restrictions of the manufacturer or distributor. Evidence of this is already showing up in customers "opinion," where more and more eBay buyers are feeling like the good deals are gone (i.e. the sellers have to sell at MAP and therefore the prices

---

34. This listing was removed October 6, 2004, and my e-mails to the contact listed (a Southern California law firm hired by McIntosh) were not returned until October 27, 2004.

35. Apparently, while the Copyright Act does limit damages if no copyright notice appears, the right to control reproduction is not affected by whether or not there is a notice. In other words, you cannot take a photo from the Web without permission—even if the Web site owner has no copyright notice. You can get photos either for free or a small charge—see www.gettyimages.com and www.inmagine.com as two places to start.

are higher). If selling new items, you have two choices: you can either sell them as "slightly used," "demo," or floor models; alternatively, you can skirt the rules and risk having your auctions closed by eBay and then you'd have to switch your product niche. You don't need the stress—you're moving to Maui, right? To conclude, plan from the start on putting your own "house brand" on products you plan to sell.

Single Versus Multiple Product Lines

You also need to decide whether you will have a business that sells multiple product brands or instead have a business that sells only its own house brand.

Here's the difference: a local sunglasses store sells 27 brands of sunglasses from six manufacturers.[36] I would strongly discourage this many choices online, but you could effectively have a Jacuzzi store that sells three different brand names—all names you have created for different price points—or perhaps two house brands and one brand that allows you to sell online and may give your business credibility. For instance, let's say you decide to sell three brands of wave runners: the Good model is Chinese-made generic, the Better is Japanese-made generic, and the Best is Yamaha. It is a viable strategy to sell Yamaha legitimately and at their MAP—and use the Yamaha name to draw in buyers via Google AdWords.

Alternatively, you could have a single brand of Jacuzzi that carries the same name as your business. This strategy assumes that your customers don't really care who made the item, but rather they buy for another reason (like price or ease of the purchase process). Old Navy sells shirts with their name, not the name of the manufacturer.

If you are having trouble with this decision, consider keeping it simple.

---

36.   Based on a conversation with the assistant store manager at a Sunglasses Hut in Folsom, CA, on October 25, 2004.

Quality

The simple fact of the matter is that for almost any product you buy, quality is good enough.

Therefore, unless you are a product leader, you should not focus on product quality as a differentiating factor. You will be a low-cost leader. When customers buy product from a low-cost leader (like Wal-Mart), those customers do not expect top quality. You as the seller need only provide passable, good quality. Note that service of the product will most likely be the responsibility of the customer in their local market. It is just too difficult to tune a piano, fix a Jacuzzi crack, or refinish a pool table post remotely. There may be individual exceptions: for instance, I know a guy from California who started a business inspecting cars that buyers found on eBay. A buyer would find a car they liked and hire this business to outsource a local inspection based upon a pre-defined list of items. It's a great idea, but now the founder is selling real-estate, so perhaps it wasn't a sustainable idea or business model.

New versus Used

Used items can have higher margins than new, because used items are harder to price-compare and acquisition cost can vary—which gives you a possible advantage. In an obvious parallel, car dealers (at least in the U.S.) make more money on used cars than new. However, selling used goods means you need detailed photographs and descriptions of each item. This raises your costs and risks and effort-level, plain and simple.

To mitigate the higher costs and effort, you need to optimize the photography processes. You could get a time advantage here if you photograph the items in the country of acquisition. For instance, if you're acquiring French antiques, take pictures of them in France before the items are loaded into the container. That way, the items can be catalogued and even sold before they reach your warehouse. Good photos are obviously important to the final sales price, and you should manage the lighting area with a professional setup. Try www.clouddome.com as an example of a portable, affordable photography studio. Managing the photos and upload process is also time-consuming (and therefore profit-reducing), so once you get the basic process down, try managing your photos and uploads with software such as the offerings from www.listd.com and www.listqueue.com.

Finally, a key to avoiding cost-overruns is to avoid returns. Returns happen when the customer's expectations aren't met; therefore, I find that slightly under-representing a used item's condition is helpful if not critical. This would account for someone's overly-high expectations or slight shipping scratches.

Selling new items avoids much of these hassles; you get one set of stock photos that you can use all the time; the descriptions don't change much; and you can quickly relist items that didn't sell the first time. If you're buying new items in China, you can easily have the manufacturer prepare the items for proper shipping, such as putting a small wooden pallet on the bottom of each item, which greatly facilitates moving in the warehouse and damage by the fork-lift. This process is illustrated in great detail later in *Maui CEO*.

Speaking of fork-lifts, let's examine some pricing data from eBay.com. In May 2007, here's what new and used forklift sales and looked like:

New forklifts: ASP = $4,461, Sell-through percentage is 29%.
Used forklifts: ASP = $1,630, Sell-through percentage is 75%.

It's likely that if you follow the Maui CEO process, the pricing spreads will be similar to those above. Expanding the timeframe a bit, here's what Rolex watches sold for between March 30 and June 27, 2007 (sorting out fakes below $500):

New Rolex watches: ASP=$5,385, 1,052 listings, 543 successful, sell-through 51.6%

Used Rolex watches: ASP=$3,287, 36 listings, 22 successful, sell-through 61.6%

In conclusion, whether you sell new or used product really depends on the product itself; whether you can "refurbish" the used product to an appropriate standard in a consistent manner; and whether the challenge of selling used is rewarded in higher product margin. In order to help you make this assessment, I am offering an eBay Sales Assistant tool on maui-ceo.com. Check it out when you get a chance.

Segmentation and Target Customer: Businesses or Individual Consumers

A 2004 episode of "The Apprentice" had Donald Trump touting the importance of knowing your customer.[37] Even the Alfred Sloan professor at MIT's Sloan School of Management encourages customer intimacy above almost all else[38]. In our situation, at this point, I don't want you to spend too much time focusing on your target customer. Identifying demographics and grouping your customers based on a segmentation scheme is not necessary right now. You might disagree. If I told you your target customer was a 51-year-old white pool player with an annual income of $58,300, how does that data change your decision-making? It doesn't, at least not yet.

Rather, what you do need to decide is whether you will target either businesses ("B to B") or consumers ("B to C"). Stating the obvious, dealing with and selling to a business is quite different from selling to a single consumer. B to B transaction sizes tend to be at least ten times larger than a consumer transaction—which means your capital costs are going to be higher. In other words, in order for you to sell a store ten Jacuzzis, you will need to have the money to buy that many (and more). Profit margins, in

---

37.   Episode 6, Season 2, aired on Thursday October 14, 2004.
38.   See *The Delta Project: Discovering New Sources of Profitability in a Networked Economy.*

my mind, are about the same between the two models, given the commoditization on the consumer side by eBay. Businesses will have different expectations of post-sale service, availability of credit and floor-financing, and even fulfillment and delivery requirements.

In order to decide whether you will target businesses or consumers, you need to estimate which is more profitable and whether you have the appropriate capital to target businesses initially. Take refurbished PCs,[39] for instance. On eBay, a sample search found a lot of 10 IBM Netvista 2.4 Ghz personal computers for sale at a unit cost of $355 each (plus $20 each for shipping). This is a lot of PCs for sale, targeted to businesses. The same company is selling an individual unit for $365 each and $23 shipping. Also consider that a different vendor is offering a very similar machine for $479 with free UPS ground shipping. Assuming these auctions represent valid ASPs, what conclusions can you draw when you decide to form your business?

Assume it costs you $20 to process each transaction. Also assume that your unit cost is $300 when buying a container full. In this realistic scenario, the first part of the financial analysis is to sell your widgets to businesses, because the higher profit on sales to individual consumers ($10, or $100 total) is offset by the higher transaction costs of processing each transaction ($20 each, or $200 total). So you would make $100 more by selling to businesses than individual consumers.

For the second step of your financial analysis, you should also try to estimate your turnover rate—in other words, how often you rotate or sell your inventory. Selling to businesses with higher margin—but lower frequency—can yield lower returns over the course of a year. For illustration, earning 40% gross profit margin selling your inventory 3 times per year means a 120% annual return on capital invested in inventory (ROCII). In contrast, earning a lower margin on your inventory (say 28%) while simultaneously turning your inventory 5 times per year means the same

39.   EBay search performed Tuesday, October 19, 2004, at 12:30 p.m. PST.

ROCII—120%. In other words, just because you may earn less margin selling to consumers, the lower margin can be offset with the accompanying higher volume.

Ever wish you could have real-time pricing history from actual eBay sales? Want to know what your target price is in China? See www.mauiceo.com.

If, after this general guidance, you still cannot decide whether you should target consumers or businesses, I suggest targeting consumers first. Then, after you work out the kinks in the processes and start to earn a little money, you can reconsider targeting businesses. In the offline world, retained customers are empirically cheaper to keep than gaining new customers. However, in the new networked economy—our world that we're creating together—we are not striving for repeat business.

This is a change in mindset for many. Most customers don't buy two or more pianos, Jacuzzis, or pool tables. It is critical to have goodwill from paying customers which translates into word-of-mouth purchases from friends—this is the concept made famous by *Crossing the Chasm*[40] and we will discuss this in the context of post-sale communication. But for now, let's figure out your business name and identity.

---

40.   Geoffrey A. Moore. *Crossing the Chasm*. Collins, 2002.

3

Developing Your Corporate Identity

This chapter discusses coming up with your business name, logo, letterhead, URL, and e-mail accounts.

I mentioned early on that *Maui CEO* is your project plan; therefore, I want to stress that chapters 3, 4 and 5 need to be happening about the same time. For instance, you might realize that you want to schedule factory visits in China to coincide with a Global Sources trade show. This will all be explained in chapter 5; stay with me. If that trade show is one month from now, you need to get busy, fast. If, however, the next trade show is four months away, then you're OK to do the activities in these three chapters sequentially.

Now that you know (or have a good idea about) which product you're going to sell, you need a few additional things. First, you need a business name; second, a logo that you can use on your Web site and letterhead; and third, a Web address (URL) to register (and possibly trademark).

Naming a business is a time-consuming process. You may already have a name in mind, but for many reasons, that name may not make sense. For instance, one of my students had an online business named Cool Stuff For You. This name may be appropriate for a one-store off-line business in a small town, but is not right for our type of online business. The most obvious weakness is the URL (Uniform Resource Locator). To find this business, what does a customer type? The business name has more than one logical way to be spelled.

www.coolstuff4u.com
or
www.coolstuff4you.com
or
www.coolstufffouryou.com
or
www.coolstufforu.com

Of course, the business owner can buy all of these Web addresses, assuming availability, and then use a feature called *domain forwarding* so that any and all variations a customer might type end up at the right Web home page. This scenario is really more trouble than it's worth. The business name should not lend itself to multiple spellings. Also, try to keep in mind a global audience. While most customers will come to you through Google or MSN, business names that are shorter and easier are preferred.

Another key characteristic of good business names is having an appropriate word connotation, based on the root or roots of the word. For instance, the name *Intel* is derived from the words *__integrated__ __electronics__*. When the name *Intel* is heard by a customer, the customer could subconsciously think of the following associations: "integrated electronics," "intelligence" or "intelligent"—all thoughts with positive and appropriate connotations.

These positive connotations can successfully be tied to your brand identity and differentiation. For illustration, a piano-seller might want to target piano students. Students tend to have lots of sheet music spread out on the music rack—or maybe even a flat-panel screen if the music is digitized—so the piano-seller would have only large, sturdy music racks on all pianos instead of the flimsy racks of competitors. Further, students tend to have teachers sitting next to them during practice or rehearsal. So the piano-seller would only include piano benches large enough for two persons.

Make sense? This seller is differentiating their product with large music racks and two-person benches. When coming up with a business name for this student piano with large music racks and duet-sized piano benches, *Sorbonne* is a good choice. Sorbonne is the name of a famous university in Paris. The name of a well-known university has the student-teacher connotation consistent with this seller's product differentiation. In fact, positioning the piano as French-made is not a bad idea, either.

Therefore, your name ideally would be consistent with either your product and/or your point of differentiation.[41] That point of differentiation could be a product feature or even the channel itself. Old Navy t-shirts, for instance, carry the name of the business instead of manufacturer.

With these tips in mind, you are now ready to contact a brand identity company to help you with the following:

- Come up with a business name consistent with the processes I've described
- Check your name choices for federal trademark availability[42]
- Design your logo for use on letterhead, envelopes, and your homepage
- Get your Web site navigation designed

Getting the federal trademark is fairly important to protect yourself in case someone else starts using your business name at the same time. "Trademark-factory" attorneys can be retained to process your federal trademark application for around $400.

---

41. For a great treatment on business naming, see *The 22 Laws of Branding*, by Al Ries and Laura Ries (HarperBusiness 2002).
42. Getting the federal trademark is fairly important to protect yourself in case someone else starts using your business name at the same time. "Trademark-factory" attorneys can be retained to process your federal trademark application for around $400.

Developing a corporate identity is a good place for you to spend a little money. I have a clear favorite recommendation here:[43] www.brandmother.com. These guys know what they're doing, are based in California, and the company is designed from the ground up to work with clients remotely. Prices are extremely reasonable, and turn-around time expectations can be agreed upon easily. If you want to shop around for these services, try a Google search for *business branding* or *logo design*. Guru.com and Elance.com are also great places where you can find fixed-priced services or use this book to outline your requirements and get competing bids.

Guru.com: The world's largest online marketplace for freelance talent.

One note about your Web site: I prefer that you get a semi-custom Web site design instead of using design templates available from your hosting company. The design templates offer limited flexibility, particularly when integrating the database. eBay's ProStores is another example; I am not

---

43.   I am a member of the Board of Advisors of LogoLab, a subsidiary of BrandMother.

sold on them either. In contrast, a semi-custom website uses a logical navigational template, but customization in other ways.

Database Design

Designing your database is probably the most difficult task you will face prior to launching your business. The best way to go about this is to have your brand identity company refer you to a database programmer. Another approach is to outsource your development to a bidder on www.rentacoder.com, www.guru.com, or www.elance.com.[44] Here you post a free description of what you want developed, programmers bid on the project, you select the best choice, and the code gets written. I outsourced www.mauiceo.com to a provider on Elance.com, and by way of reference, received an average bid of $1201. Escrow keeps a third party between you, the coder, and the money.

One thing to remember as a goal is to have the database structure done **before** the Web site is finalized. The Web site design, other than the home page and core navigation, must support how content (inventory, photos, blogs) is delivered to the customer. The Web site pages must also support the checkout process, as managed by the database design.

To collect payment, you have three options: get a merchant account and process credit cards through Verisign; integrate with PayPal; or integrate with Escrow.com[45]. Getting a merchant account is best done through an organization. For instance, if you belong to the National Association of Music Merchants,[46] they have prenegotiated Visa and Mastercard rates with a bank (in this case, First National Bank of Omaha). Rates charged to

---

44. If you want a personal recommendation, and can afford $150 per hour, contact Douglas Technology Consulting at 916.752.6849. Their expertise is in .net and c-sharp, but they can also program in Microsoft Access and Macromedia ColdFusion. Otherwise, I like Indian firm ebizzsol on Elance.com, whose fees run closer to $15 per hour.

45. See www.escrow.com

46. See http://www.namm.com

you are typically 2.3% of the purchase price, with American Express and Discover being closer to 3.1%. Then you have your database designer set up a "CGI Script" or gateway between your Web site and Verisign. This allows your customer information to be automatically transferred from you to Verisign, so that the customer does not have to retype their information. The credit card charge is run, approved, and then your Web site generates a receipt.

An easier approach is to use PayPal merchant services,[47] which basically accomplishes the same thing. Charges might be a bit higher than the 2.3% friends and family rate described above, but you can certainly get going faster through PayPal. After a year or two, you can use your sales records to go to your local bank and see if you can get a better rate. Remember, your average transaction size is going to be much larger than everyone else's size, which is incentive for the bank to give you a lower merchant rate.

The third approach I mentioned is to integrate with Escrow.com. The pay process is very similar to the one described with PayPal above, except that the escrow company holds payment until the merchandise is received by the buyer. The process is similar technically to PayPal—the business sets up a gateway between their site and escrow to manage the flow of information and transaction completion.

Both PayPal and Escrow are described in detail in later chapters, primarily Chapter 10.

Everything must come in its true order, grasshopper.

URL Acquisition

Your brand identity company will obviously check for the availability of the URL. For instance, if you come up with *Veritas* as one of your com-

---

47.   See http://www.paypal.com/cgi-bin/webscr?cmd=_merchant-outside

pany name possibilities, that name cannot be chosen as a finalist until you know that the URL can be registered by you.

Although there is good competition, I believe the best place to do this registration is www.domainsinseconds.com. They will show you the contact information for every domain that is already registered. Just click on their click here for info link and see if the owner is interested in letting the domain name go for cheap.

Of course your brand identity company will check on the names you're considering. Once you decide upon a name,

- consider all spelling possibilities,
- register those alternative spellings, and

- use domain forwarding and URL keeper features to transfer those alternative spellings to the right homepage.

For instance, Barnes & Noble's actual homepage is www. barnesandnoble.com. However, an alternative spelling (and one they use on collateral) is www.bn.com. Type www.bn.com and you are automatically transferred to www.barnesandnoble.com.[48]

As a side note, I don't really believe that you should try to buy all possible extensions, namely .com, .net, and .biz. The reason is because most people in the future will find you through a search engine and save you as a bookmark anyway. One argument in favor of buying all possible extensions is the proliferation of spoofing, which means Web users will eventually grow overly leery of following embedded links in e-mail. For example, instead of following a link in an eBay e-mail, to open up your PayPal account, you should open a new window altogether and type www.paypal.com. If PayPal were legitimately a .net extension, such as www.concast.net, then some customers will naturally confuse .net with .com. I discuss spoofing in chapter 10.

E-Mail Accounts

Once you have finalized a business name, it is time to open up your e-mail accounts. I recommend the following structure: these are in the format [info@bizname.com, status@bizname.com] and so on.

- Info: the general account to which 90% of company e-mail comes

- Status: where customers send requests for fulfillment and delivery status

- Spoof: this is a new trend where customers can forward e-mails to confirm the e-mail's authenticity[49]

---

48. As an example of bad naming, the *&* is not a valid domain name server (DNS) character. Therefore, if someone types www.barnes&noble.com in the address line, an error is returned.
49. For a tutorial on spoofing, see http://pages.ebay.com/education/spooftutorial/.

Then, you setup an e-mail account for each employee using their first name: terri@company.com, jake@company.com, and so on. All of these email accounts are easily setup in your hosting account. Your host like also has new anti-spam software—all included in their hosting price.

Skype Accounts

While you are at it, you might as well set up your Skype telephone service now. Skype is a small piece of software that lets you use your computer (and specially-designed phones) to make phone calls over the internet. You can call to China or India for 2-3 cents per minute ... incredible value and incredibly valuable. Download the small business version here: http://www.skype.com/business/ for free. The small business version lets you get a master account and pay for credit there, and each employee gets an account that points to the master but has separate tracking, etc. That way, if an employee leaves your employ, you still maintain control of the account.

4

Establishing Your Corporate Structure

For most businesses, the ideal corporate structure is to incorporate in Nevada. Want to incorporate for $300? I tell you how.

There are numerous resources for deciding on which format—or structure—your new business should take. The starting-your-own-business dummy guides are good places to find supplemental data.

That said, I believe you should structure most product businesses—the kind we have been discussing—as Nevada C Corporations. Of course, you should and must consult your tax advisor and perform due diligence on this topic. I am not a practicing attorney and this is not tax or legal advice.

Quick Introduction to Corporate Structure

You can set up your business as a sole proprietorship or as some type of corporation. Sole proprietorships are good for home-based businesses. You can "write off" a fair number of expenses, run your business so that it shows a small loss on paper (hey—the Italians do it), and pass that loss directly to your own Form 1040. The paperwork required to have a sole proprietorship structure around your business is marginal.

The downside, of course, is a higher level of liability from your business activities. Consider what this legal liability means. For instance, if you ship

35

someone a large playground set—which is damaged in shipping—what is the true extent of your legal liability? In reality, you can just ship another unit and reduce chance of litigation. That said, it should be noted that from a tax standpoint the "word on the street" is that sole proprietorships have a much higher chance of IRS audit.[50]

In contrast, many business owners like the prestige of having and saying they own their own "company." You should be aware that regardless of a company's profit or loss, that company will owe a minimum of $600-$800 in franchise taxes every year. In other words, even if your corporate entity loses $10,000, you will still owe $800 in taxes on Form 541. As a general rule, then, your business needs about $60,000 in revenue to break-even (covering the $800 in franchise taxes).

Why a C Corporation?

All corporations start as Cs, and the other options like S Corporations and Limited Liability Corporations are variations on the C theme. All are good choices—the difficulty is deciding which structure is best for your particular business.

The best way to describe "why C?" is that C has more benefits to our ends than the other competing formats. First, there is more legal precedent on the C Corporation than other formats. This is an advantage in that I would much rather have an attorney tell me: "You will lose this hearing because of X, Y, and Z" rather than the attorney saying, "There is no LLC case-law on the subject." Case law and administrative rulings provide good evidence of how a court or agency would rule on an issue.

Second, in order for the benefits of the S corporate structure to be applied, business information is provided to the IRS. In other words, for you and

50. According to some collateral from one of the incorporation services, "Sole proprietorships...are the highest audited business structures...[and] corporations have a less than 2% chance of being audited by the IRS." *Incorporate In Tax Free Nevada*, Laughlin International, Inc. of Carson City, NV, pg 2.

your two partners to carry one third of the S-Corp loss to your personal tax returns, all of that information goes on each person's return. This severely weakens our desire for privacy and protection (see note on Nevada below and the latest organizational strategies). The number of partners/members is limited in S Corporations and LLCs, whereas the C Corporations' stock gives you scalable flexibility.

Third, the C Corporation is treated as a separate entity, and therefore is taxed differently and separately from you. Corporate tax rates are lower than individual tax rates, and of course corporations are entitled to many tax deductions that are not available to sole proprietorships or partnerships. This may include season tickets and more generous automobile and travel allowances.

How To Structure Now In Case of Bankruptcy Later

Finally, a Corporation gives you something your sole proprietorship cannot: your money back if you file for bankruptcy. The magic happens in three places: first, when your attorney issues stock, make sure it is called "Section 1244" stock; second, in the appropriate location such as your first board of director meeting minutes and on the stock certificate, say the magic words "Section 1244" stock; and third, if your company loses money and closes, including bankruptcy, you file Federal Form 4797 "Sale of Business Property." Your loss is counted as "Ordinary" and will have the accompanying favorable tax treatment. If your loss of investment is $90,000, you won't get it all back, but it will make your Form 1040 look incredibly better! In the spirit of this book's practicality, here is my non-legal, non-tax advice on what to say:

- First, in your incorporation papers, say "I, [your name], hereby assign to [name of company] the assets described on Exhibit "A" attached hereto and incorporated herein at the values stated therein in exchange for 25,000 shares of common stock of [name of company].

- Second, in your first "Minutes of the first meeting of the Board of Directors of [name of company]," note something like the following: "<u>Section 1244 Stock</u>. The Board of Directors have determined that in order to attract investment in the Corporation the Corporation shall be organized and managed so that it is a "small business corporation" as defined by Internal Revenue Code Section 1244(c)(1), as amended, and so that the shares issued by the Corporation are "Section 1244 stock" as defined in Internal Revenue Code Section 1244(c)(1), as amended. Compliance with this section will enable shareholders to treat the loss on the sale or exchange of their shares as an "ordinary loss" on their personal income tax returns. RESOLVED, that the proper officers of the Corporation are authorized to sell and issue common shares in an aggregate amount of money and other property (as a contribution to capital and as paid up in surplus), which together with the aggregate amount of common shares outstanding at the time of issuance does not exceed one mission dollars, and RESOLVED, that the sale and issuance of shares shall be conducted in compliance with Internal Revenue Code Section 1244, so that the Corporation and its shareholders may obtain the benefits of Internal Revenue Code Section 1244, and RESOLVED FURTHER, that the proper officers of the Corporation are directed to maintain such accounting records as are necessary so that any shareholder that experiences a loss on the transfer of common shares of the Corporation may determine whether they qualify for "ordinary loss" deduction treatment on their personal income tax returns."

Your particular business or situation may lead you to conclude that you should incorporate as an LLC or S Corporation (or not at all). That's fine. The following advice applies to all corporate structures.

Why Form in Nevada

The reasons for using Nevada are many, and these reasons range from simple to complex.

First, it is believed that at least half of new Nevada incorporations are by individuals from other states.[51] Second, Nevada has no income tax, no tax on corporate shares, no franchise tax, and so on. As noted earlier, even Nevada corporation still have to pay *federal* franchise taxes. Third, Nevada is apparently the only U.S. state that does not share information with the IRS. Despite tightening of requirements in May 2007 to cut down on money-laundering and criminal activity, the key benefits remain. The net result of these benefits is no taxes and higher privacy for you.

One person in Nevada can hold corporate positions, so the same person can be treasurer and secretary, for instance. The corporate officers (i.e., treasurer) can live anywhere in the world. You can have board meetings in Hawaii, for instance. You can incorporate with the assistance of an incorporation service and never set foot in the state.

If your business starts to become successful, then you can take further steps to "bullet-proof" your corporation's legality through the services of incorporation services.[52]

How to Incorporate for $300

When the first edition of *Maui* CEO was published, there were only five Nevada-based companies that could assist you with incorporation. Now they are coming out of the woodwork. My recommendation is to use Inc Paradise (http://www.incparadise.com/). At time of writing, Inc Paradise will incorporate you in Nevada for $283. This fee includes everything, including filing fee, stamped articles, name availability check, and resident agent for a year (required). Also, for $168[53] this company will also give you a 90-120 minute consultation on selecting the right structure.

---

51. *Incorporate In Tax Free Nevada*, Laughlin International, Inc. of Carson City, NV, pg 3.

52. See http://123-inc.com/, http://www.companiesinc.com/, or http://www.nevadaincorporation.org/

53. http://www.incparadise.com/asset-protection/

The Inc Paradise Web site also provides links and information on setting up a local bank account (if required), mail forwarding, getting a free Employer Identification Number (EIN) and local phone numbers. Inc Paradise can be reached at the URL above or at 1.888.284.3821. As an alternative, investigate Biz Filings at www.bizfilings.com. I have not used their services, but they do spend money to have a booth at eBay Live, so that is promising.

If you need fancier things, like having a live operator answer the Nevada phone number with your business name, then you should also consider Laughlin Associates. Laughlin is well-respected and provides incorporation services in all 50 states. See www.laughlininternational.com or call 1.800.648.0966.

The Latest Strategy

Many accountants and merchant bankers[54] will tell you not to incorporate out of state, because you can never get around the "nexus" of being in another state. This may be true, depending on the type of business you establish. However, within the context of businesses contemplated by this book, articulate to your advisers the "virtual" nature of the majority of your activities. You are targeting 48 States, not a local community.

If you are still worried, here's the latest tax reduction strategy: set up a C Corporation in one state and an S Corporation in Nevada.

---

54. A merchant banker is a fancy word for someone who helps $5M-$20M businesses get non-traditional funding outside of venture capital.

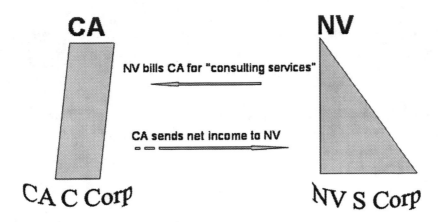

CA **NV**

NV bills CA for "consulting services"

CA sends net income to NV

CA C Corp   NV S Corp

Let's say you "live" in Nevada, either physically or through an incorporation services' "residence" program. You also lease warehouse space in California, and therefore feel a nexus requirement to California.

First, you set up a C Corporation in California. Any activity which appears to be California-based is directed to and through this company. This company is named, has a website, and so on. The C Corporation structure provides a few extra barriers between you and the corporate organization.

Second, you set up a Nevada S Corporation. This is named XYZ Corp., or something that can in no way be easily connected to the California C Corporation.

Now, let's assume the California C Corporation makes $200,000. They set up a consulting agreement with the Nevada S Corporation for $200,000 of periodic payments. In this manner, the $200,000 of profits are drained from California to Nevada. In California, you have $0 net profit and therefore pay no CA income taxes. Once the $200,000 is in Nevada, which has no state income tax, you have saved yourself 9%-10%. Then, pay yourself a small salary (say, $50,000) or take distributions as permitted by the Corporation, and use the rest to pay against corporate bills.

Obviously, this type of dual-state structure requires that both corporate entities pay the minimum franchise taxes, which means the break-even is around $120,000 of gross income.

Again, I am not encouraging you to do anything blatantly illegal. As you focus on your low-cost value proposition, no cow is sacred, meaning every way to reduce costs must be considered.

For now, we move from Nevada to China.

This website is maintained by Runckel & Associates, a consulting firm based in Portland, Oregon. Look for the comprehensive content on Shanghai China and Thailand, in particular, to bulk up your knowledge in this space. After reviewing this information, you are ready to explore your manufacturing options. Remember: when you start out, buy a ready-made product. You are not trying to design your own product yet!

Finding a Chinese Manufacturer Through A Consultant

There are several companies advertising their services to help you find a factory in China. The advantage of this process is that you aren't going into something by yourself. These consultants or their companies have some contacts in China; turn-around times might be adequate; and, in principle, you have a third-party to mediate problems.

I did a Google search for "finding a factory in China" and got several interesting results. Search engine results are always changing, so make sure you check out

www.globalsources.com
and
www.china-synergy.org

The downside to these types of arrangements is obvious: if you can find a contact this way, so too can your competition. Also, while your prices may be low, you are trying to be the low-cost **leader**. Set the goal to have a most favored customer ("MFC") clause in your eventual contract. An MFC clause says that if the manufacturer offers anyone else pricing better than yours, then the same pricing is automatically passed to you. An MFC clause may not be readily available until you are a better customer, but it never hurts to ask. I have successfully negotiated this clause three times in different situations. Remember that you are looking for any way to assert a long-term cost advantage.

Finding A Chinese Manufacturer Through a Tradeshow

To truly get your product cheaply, I recommend that you find a Chinese manufacturer at a tradeshow. Here's what you do:

- Visit your industry's tradeshow in China

   o In other words, if you sell tubas, you want to attend the musical industry's tradeshow in China. This is where you can compare and contrast your options

   o Companies that sell tradeshow booths may be able to help you here

   o See also www.tradeshow.globalsources.com. These guys also maintain a booth at eBay Live, and attract lots of attention. However, they will try to get you to buy from their network of suppliers—which in my mind makes them the middleman and defeats the purpose of flying all the way over there! Global sources has tradeshows in China, Hong Kong, and even Dubai, and these can have different themes, such as Home Products.

- Get the tradeshow schedule from the Shanghai Mart. This is where most of the best tradeshows are held in Shanghai China. See www.shanghaimart.com

As a side note, I'd recommend staying at the Sheraton Grand Tai Ping Yang Hotel. This beautiful place is only a few minute walk to the Shanghai Mart; has a wonderful English-speaking staff; has a nice lobby area to meet vendors; and, most importantly, has a Starbucks Coffee down the street! Also, don't forget that proper credentials are generally required to get into that tradeshow.

When you get to the tradeshow,

- have lots of business cards, preferably with your information in Chinese on the back[57]

---

57.   Try http://www.lunaconcepts.com/e/biz/index.html.

- read up on proper etiquette;
- consider hiring an interpreter[58];
- ask for price lists;
- be prepared to say you're considering ordering a 20-foot container full of their product;
- realize that if your picture gets taken with some of the exhibitors, these exhibitors plan on putting the picture on their website showing you as their "partner," which may hurt you later; and
- focus on talking to the exhibitors who do not have a Caucasian in the booth.

On this last point, our plan is to buy product from someone who does not already have a U.S. distributor. If the Chinese company already has a U.S. distributor, then you might be subject to paying a price no lower than the price provided to everyone else. Also, if there is already a U.S. distributor, that organization becomes very protective of their Chinese counterparts. Once you find a vendor or two who can sell you what you need, you're ready to order your first container.

---

58. Consider http://www.patw-china-consultant.com/china_translator_interpreter. htm

6

How to Order Your First Container From China

This chapter outlines getting a good deal on shipping your container, processing international payment, finding a customs broker, and determining import duties.

Assume that you went to the Shanghai tradeshow and got some confidential, wholesale pricelists. Now what?

First, remember that quoted prices are likely Freight On Board (FOB). FOB is a price structure which includes loading of product into a container and making the container ready to ship. Depending on the manufacturer, their FOB price may or may not include container transportation between the factory and the local port. The term used by manufacturers in this situation is "ex works." Ex means "from," and works means "factory." Even though the company may load the container for free at their factory, if things go bad between you and the company and the quote is ex works, the company could charge you a loading fee. Of course, your effort is reduced if the price quoted gets the container to the port.

To make things even easier, ask for a Cost Insurance Freight (CIF) quote. As the title suggests, this quotation includes not only the cost (the "FOB price"), but also insurance and container freight charges across the ocean to your home port.

Also, in most situations getting a quote (and paying for the merchandise) in U.S.dollars is to your advantage. Despite the buy-sell currency rates you see in the newspapers, your rates will be less advantageous. For instance, if the Yen to Dollar ratio is 115, your effective rate will be closer to 105. This hurts your bottom line. If the seller will quote in dollars and accepts dollar transfers, then the currency risk is really on their shoulders.

If the manufacturer offers and you accept a CIF quotation, your involvement is pretty much limited to when the container arrives in the destination port. In a CIF scenario, here are a few additional recommendations:

- Insure your cargo for 110% of its FOB value.
- Have the documentation expedited to you once the container has disembarked.
- Ask for two copies of the original Bill of Lading.

The documentation sent to you will include: a) Invoice; b) Bill of Lading; and c) proof of insurance. You will need to send the invoice and original Bill of Lading to your customs broker. I discuss the customs broker later in this chapter, but for now, realize that your broker is U.S.-based and helps get your container through customs. File your proof of insurance certificate in a safe place. I once had a container of merchandise arrive inexplicably scratched—and the insurance claim was easy. I hired a repairman, then faxes his bill to the insurance company, and was quickly reimbursed.

Finding a Company To Transport Your Container—How to Get a Good Deal

As I described above, selecting a CIF quote is easier than accepting the FOB price and then arranging for your own container shipping. However, a lower total cost is typically found by arranging for your own container shipping. For many of you, this means getting third-party quotes from Shanghai, China to Long Beach, California. By the way, Long Beach and Los Angeles are separate ports, but treated virtually the same both by the companies quoting you a price, and by your customs broker charging for the short "drayage" or container transport distance from port to ware-house.

Here is my recommended starting place for getting container quotes:

1. Start at Fedex.com and go to Freight Services. Click on the Ocean Freight tab. From their, you can request a quote.

2. Do a Google search of "freight forwarder." Based on the search results, get container shipping quotes from a number of vendors. Remember that vendors are much more willing to quote businesses than individuals.

3. Visit Hanjin Shipping at www.hanjin.com. Hanjin is a market leader in this space.

4. For an instant quote from a portal, see www. freight-calculator.com

Here are some representative quotes I was able to procure in Summer and Fall 2004. Unless noted, these quotes include loading charges, the freight from Shanghai to Long Beach itself, and a few other fees. The quotes are listed in no particular order and do not come with any recommendation. Most companies have difficulty responding to your e-mail and online queries, and therefore end up requiring a phone call to get a quote.

Source	Details
www.freightforwarding.com	Quoted $2,210 for a full 20-foot container and $2865 for a full 40-foot container
FedEx Trade Networks	Quoted $2,121 for a full 20-foot container
www.allisonshipping.com	Quoted $1,700 for a full 20-foot container
www.maersksealand.com	Quoted $1,850 for a full 2-foot container
3L-Leemark Logistics	Quoted $1,850 for a full 20-foot container
www.airseaint.com	Quoted $1,800 for a full 20-foot container
www.rapidfreightinc.com	Quoted $635 for freight (not including loading charge)

Twenty foot containers are the smaller size and the most logical place to start. Shipping overhead per unit is obviously lower with a forty-foot container, which tends to hold about 90% more than a 20 foot container; however, a 40-foot container holds so much inventory for a newly minted small business, unless your business is well capitalized, I would consider selecting the 20 foot container size first. As a side note, container transport to Southern California generally takes about 10 days from Osaka Japan; about 19 days from Shanghai China; and about 28 days from Manila Philippines.

Also, an additional option is to ship less than a full-container load, alternatively known as Less-than Container Loads (LCL). In other words, you would share container space with others. The advantages and disadvantages of LCL are obvious. One quote I received, for reference only, was $1215 for 10,000 pounds of toys (about 12.5 cubic meters of space in the container).[59] Based on several sources, a standard 20-foot container holds about 49,000 lbs. Also, be aware that containers usually cost the same to ship, whether loaded with 1,000 lbs of feathers or 49,000 pounds of bricks. In other words, weight is immaterial to the cost of shipping.

If you are interested in shipping a container from the U.S. to a foreign destination, you can see rates online at <u>www.discount-shipping.net</u>.

Paying For The Container

You can pay in any number of ways. The most common methods of payment are international bank wire and international Letter of Credit. Although fees may differ from bank to bank, an international bank wire generally costs about $42. Note that your supplier may refer to a bank wire as a T/T (telegraphic transfer) or electronic transfer. The big advantage is speed. You authorize the transfer at your bank, and the money arrives in a few days. Your bank will want the suppliers' SWIFT information, which is a simple international bank identification code. The biggest downfall is

---

59.   Quote from Simon Wu, simon@gafgof.com.

that your money could be gone, if the seller goes out of business before shipping the goods.

One way to have some level of protection is to use an international letter of credit (often called an L/C). This is my recommended method for your first container order, until you build up some confidence in and a relationship with your supplier. Despite what the ivory-tower textbooks say, international letters of credit are a pain. Here's the easiest and safest way to process letters of credit:

First, give yourself plenty of time. Opening an L/C takes at least 10 business days. Second, transfer the exact amount needed into a separate bank account. Use that account number on the L/C application with your bank. When the bank issues the L/C, it is unusually common for your entire account balance to be "frozen" until the L/C is executed, even though only the amount of the L/C is supposed to be frozen. Don't forget to consider the amount of the L/C, which is commonly around $425[60]. This amount becomes egregious over time, and will eventually encourage you to either use T/T or seek some kind of trade credit with your supplier.

L/Cs are not entirely immune to fraud. I've heard of a situation where a Japanese supplier sent a container full of rocks to a Toronto buyer. Once a container clears customs, the L/C is paid by the bank—but in this case, the container was shipped by rail all the way from Vancouver to Toronto—providing more than enough time for the supplier to disappear.

One other option you might be presented with is to pay cash for a portion of your product. Here's how it works: a) fly to Asia on an inexpensive e-fare; b) carry around $20,000 in cash; c) meet a company representative, give them the cash, have a beer, and return home. Then, your invoice is reduced by $20,000, and you pay less import duties (which are assessed on your original invoice). The problem here is three-fold: first, this is illegal.

---

60. This amount becomes egregious over time, and will eventually encourage you to either use T/T or seek some kind of trade credit with your supplier.

Second, the math doesn't work in your favor. For instance, this little "mileage run" only saves you around $1,000 in duties[61]. Third, you now have to lie about cost of goods sold, or your taxes will be much higher. Avoid this transaction—the benefits do not match the costs.

To summarize, try to get CIF quotes and pay in U.S. dollars. I'd recommend using an international letter of credit until you are comfortable with your supplier(s), and then pay with T/T.

Finding and Hiring a Customs Brokers

The role of a customs broker is to get your container through customs, and to assist getting your container picked up from the port and delivered to your warehouse. Customs brokers are paid a small percentage of the invoice for their services.

For a few contacts and pricing on services, get a member of the National Customs Brokers & Forwarders Association of America, Inc. See http://www.ncbfaa.org/. I can also recommend, from personal experience, BJ Customs Brokerage Company[62].

The process of picking up your container from the port and transporting the container to your warehouse is called "drayage." A competitive price for this service, assuming your container only has to go from Long Beach to a local warehouse, is $125.

Import duties

You may have to pay the U.S. government a "duty" on the product you're importing. For illustration, if you import acoustic pianos, whether new or used, the import duty rate is 4.7%. This percentage is tacked on to your invoice total. For this reason, your customs broker gets a detailed copy of

61. $20,000 invoice discount * 4.7% duty = $940.
62. BJ Customs Brokerage is located at 5730 West Manchester Avenue, Los Angeles, CA 90045. Alternatively, you can call (310) 337-1628 and ask for Johnny Lee.

your invoice; pays the duties to the government; then invoices you for the duties, along with their service fees.

For the latest information on both duties specifically and customs generally, see the official U.S. governmental website at <u>www. customs.ustreas.gov</u>. To find out you're your product's import duty or import tariff is, do a Google search for the latest "United States Harmonized Tariff Schedule." Since import tariffs are one of the largest sources of revenue for the government, there is little incentive to classify your product correctly (in the lowest bracket). Also, customs brokers can be remarkably unknowledgeable about the duties applicable to your product. This one is up to you.

Additionally, depending on the number of containers you import, you could save significantly by paying about $500 for a 12-month customs bond.[63] Otherwise, each container you import will have a certain "bond" charge assessed through the customs broker. FedEx was able to assist me in getting my own customs bond, although your customs broker could probably also assist with this bond purchase…. or see a specialist at <u>http:// traderiskguaranty.com</u>.

Mastering Container Importation Helps You Compete and Win

By now your head is swimming. You're probably thinking "I'll just skip this part and by from Global Sources or big lots on eBay and then resell them." The choice is obviously yours, but remember that you are going to be competing against businesses with more money than you. There is a magical combination of selling large items, imported without layers of distributors, importers and middlemen. Of necessity you become something

---

63. Depending on volume of containers you import, you could save significantly by paying about $500 for a 12-month customs bond. Otherwise, each container you import will have a certain "bond" charge assessed through the customs broker. FedEx was able to assist me with getting my own customs bond.

of a logistics expert, while simultaneously raising barriers to competitors. This is rare and wonderful and key to profitability.

I can honestly tell you that the process gets easy—very easy. Once established, you get a new product; select your products from the supplier and pay; monitor the container's progress with your customs broker; and try to presell as much inventory as you can. The result is being able to sell product cheaper than competitors can buy product. Now THAT is power.

The process of finding sellers in China can take time; therefore, let's now work simultaneously on your pricing strategy and getting your website up—subjects we now turn to in Chapter 7.

7

Getting Your Website Up

We start by discussing your pricing/payment strategies and the need for interactivity. With that information in mind, we move to the fun stuff, including databases, site hosting, XML, and merchant integration.

According to Young & Rubicam, buyers don't think of the eBay brand as just shopping; instead eBay is part shopping, part Internet, and part entertainment. As you consider your website's theme and direction, consider these suggestions from eBay itself. As this book goes to print in the second edition, eBay has redesigned their front-end (using Apollo AIR) to make it more buyer-friendly. According to an internal eBay Buyer Engagement project in April 2007[64], buyers want:

- A site that is "easy to use"

- One that has updated information

- One that "loads quickly"

- A site that has relevant content, namely content which relates to why the buyer is there

- Few distractions like banner ads and pop-ups

- Variety and visually interesting content: text, video, pictures and sound

---

64. "Lessons from eBay Buyer Research," Jeff Resnick of eBay, at the 2007 eBay Developer's Conference (Boston).

These are all obvious to most of us, but bear mentioning when you're considering the high-level goals of your web presence.

Before I outline the "back-end" or database structure of your website, I want to propose a pricing strategy. Your pricing strategy needs to be thought out now, so that the specifics can be designed into your website early on.

Pricing Strategy

Economic theory offers a plethora of complicated ways to set pricing. The parameters are set by what customers will pay. In this world, you interview sample "customers" and plot demand (price willing to pay) against supply/product choice, and your economically-efficient price is where the two lines cross each other. Of course, those who can't do, teach! Alternatively, you can also analyze the pricing on eBay (for sold items), giving you actual real-world data.

You will have time later to refine your pricing strategy. For now, we need to put a stake in the ground for your web design.

Your basic pricing strategy is to target a 40% markup over cost.

To get 40%, you actually start out marking up everything by 46%. This price automatically includes escrow services. Escrow, described in great detail in the eBay/PayPal chapter, is highly favored by buyers because escrow makes buyers feel more comfortable. In stark contrast, sellers, like you, would instead prefer to get paid with a bank wire transfer.

Pricing as it Relates To How You Accept Payment

For payment, you would ideally want to accept only bank wire transfers. Why? Because the money is deposited in your account in short order. You aren't paying merchant fees, and don't have to worry about fraud to the same extent as other payment methods.

The second most desirable payment option would be, in most cases, to receive a certified bank check. This is desirable for the same reasons as the bank wire, but the downside is that two trips were made to the bank—the customer/buyer, and you! Someone has to get the check and make the deposit. This is kind of hard to do when you're in Maui! Customers don't like sending a $5,000 bank check to a Maui address, for good reason.

The third most desirable payment option is to take a credit card, and so on. As you may know, you cannot legally charge customers more if they use a credit card. However, you can charge them less! Here is my recommendation as a starting place.

Recommended Discount Structure

Payment Method	Discount Offered
Bank Wire	<5%>
Cashier's Check	<3%>
Credit Card	<2%>
Escrow	<0%>

These discounts offer incentives for customers to pay with another method other than escrow, even though you've gotten them "hooked" in part by touting how all transactions include the safety of escrow. If a customer wants escrow, they are paying you 46% gross margin, and escrow.com will take about 5% for escrow fees, leaving you with 41% margin. Regardless of how the customer pays, you are able to cover your payment fees and still hit your target gross margin of 40%. You do this by offering them a discount! Let me say this another way: all sales should include free escrow. The presence of escrow reassures buyers. Your goal, once the customer is in checkout, is to get them to "waive" escrow and pay with a bank wire, cashier's check or credit card.

Finally, I recommend offering buyers an additional 1% discount if they fill out a 10 question survey after the transaction is completed. This survey is the foundation for your customer knowledge and future marketing efforts. In my experience, this 1% discount for filling out a survey exchange has a response rate of about 85%—fantastic by any standard. I provide a sample professionally designed survey below—free of charge.

You will take this pricing structure with you into your database requirements. Let's look at the sample survey, then interactivity, and then those pesky database requirements.

Sample Online Survey

We are interested in understanding how we can enhance your online shopping experience. Please take our 2-minute survey and receive an additional 1% off your current [product] purchase.

1. How did you find us? (radio buttons)

    a.   Yahoo

    b.   Google

    c.   MSN

    d.   AOL

    e.   Other Search Engine

    f.   [Industry]

    g.   Friend/Family

    h.   E-bay

    i.   Other—*please describe*

2. Where else did you consider making your purchase before choosing [company name]? Check all that apply. (check boxes)

    a.   Start with your competition, including brick and mortar

    b.   Online competitor

3. Why did you choose [company name]? Check all that apply. (check boxes)

    a. Best Price

    b. Good Quality

    c. Good Selection

    d. Convenience of online shopping with home delivery

    e. Most informative and/or user-friendly website

    f. Friend's recommendation [type their name here]

    g. Other

4. Would you recommend [company name] to someone or purchase from us again? (radio buttons)

    a. Yes

    b. No

5. Are there any additional [product]-related items or services you are considering to purchase in the near future? (radio buttons)

    a. Yes, I'm considering: _____

    b. No

6. Gender: (radio buttons)

    a. Male

    b. Female

7. Annual household income: (radio buttons)

    a. Less than $50,000

    b. $50,000 to $100,000

    c. $100,000 to $150,000

    d. More than $150,000

8. How would you characterize the person(s) for whom the [product] is being purchased? (radio buttons)

    a. Semi-professional to professional

    b. Avid user

    c. Recreational player

    d. Just getting started

Other: _____

Interactivity

We discussed this earlier, but interactivity refers to "the interaction between the site and a user of that site[65]." Countless academic studies[66], as well as common sense, prove that interactivity is a fundamental requirement for building trust and a comfort level conducive to purchasing—especially expensive items.

I have an exercise I facilitate with my eBusiness MBA students which highlights good interactive features. I ask the students to visit 2 or 3 of their favorite websites and list desirable web features. Students routinely identify websites which include:

- Personalization (advice, product selection)
- Opt-in email (early notification of product availability, newsletter, club membership)
- 'Search the web' capability from the home page
- Clear identification of any shipping and tax charges

---

65. Hoffman, D. and Novak, T. (1996), "Marketing in hypermedia computer-mediated environments: conceptual foundations", *Journal of Marketing*, Vol. 60, pp. 50-68.

66. Merrilees, B. and Fry, M.L. (2003), "E-trust: the influence of perceived interactivity on e-retailing users", *Marketing Intelligence & Planning*, 21/2 pp. 123-128. See also Urban, G.L., Sultan, F. and Qualls, W.J. (2000), "Placing trust at the center of your Internet strategy", *Sloan Management Review*, Fall, pp. 39-48.

When you think of interactivity, I recommend you concentrate on creating virtual two-way communication. For instance, the shopper can give you a little information (like their ZIP or country code), and you give them information back ("free shipping to this city/state until Feb 15"). The visitor tells you what they are looking for ("10,000 gallon Koi pond"), and you send them an email telling them what your inventory will be before the data reaches the website. The customer wants to review your returns policy—and you provide it quickly (or email it to them). Since we're not trying to create a social network, there's no need to overdo it here. You're not trying to win the "most interactive" website award. Along with the other suggestions mentioned earlier in the first paragraph of this chapter, keep your website sharp, crisp and professional, and don't bury your shopping cart. Your home page should load in six to eight seconds (no longer!), and the customer should be able to have an item in their cart in three clicks.

With the baselines of pricing, payment and interactivity set, let's now review the database requirements.

Database Requirements

As I stated earlier in the book, you should have the database done **before** the website is finalized. The database can be "turn-key," meaning that you are using a generic database and shopping cart combination. A more sophisticated, but pre-packaged, shopping cart solution would be illustrated by the products offered by www.storefront.net.

Alternatively, you can outsource exactly what you want to either a local database programmer or someone you find on one of the indexes I referred to earlier, such as www.elance.com (recommended!). In all scenarios, here are my guidelines for acquiring a software developer. Note: if you are non-technical, you may have to read this section several times.

Formalize Specifications Up Front

The one thing that software developers and their clients don't like is to find out in the middle of a project that the specifications given in the beginning are incomplete or don't meet the business needs. If you've ever remodeled your kitchen or house, and made changes along the way, you know what I mean: people get frustrated and costs escalate quickly.

Therefore, you should have a good idea of how the software will flow and the kind of data that it will need to keep and process. In other words, first create a design document that clearly spells out the business and technical requirements. Describe the business needs early, so the developer will understand your business. Describe the problems that the software needs to solve or how the software will help the business achieve its goals. Create pictures of your web pages and flow charts to show the developer how the application should work.

As an example, here is the actual text I used to attract bidders to this book's website:

> ### *Title: Project Description for Website with Blog, PayPal, and API calling capabilities*
>
> I am looking for a website which highlights my book. This book was published in 2005 and I am just completing a second edition. See www.mauiceo.com, which I created as a placeholder. The book won two awards and I would like to highlight both of them (Editor's Choice and Reader's Choice from iUniverse.com).
>
> **Objective of the website**: 1) support the themes of the book *Maui CEO* as described below; 2) sell eBay research services; and 3) foster a sense of community through blogging.
>
> The book's story line is about leaving your day job and start-ing your own business wherever you live (like Maui). Key topics are China or India, import/export, containers or container ships, ware-houses, and eBay. I would therefore want the website to be consistent

with these themes, as appropriate. I can provide you an image of the book's cover (which I paid for via license); the other images used on the website would need to be license/royalty free unless some image was so good and necessary, it would be worth paying for.

Here are my ideas about the website pages; the bolded name is the navigational title:

Home—clean, professional, up-to-date look. Site search capability.

Welcome and Executive Summary—Summary of book and a 30-second video—based welcome from me which I will provide.

Testimonials—text-based quotes. I'm not sure how to make this page exciting ... perhaps we can have a "Submit your testimonial" option?

About the Author—text and photos, as well as the following options:
eBay Sales Assistant
I anticipate this to be four webpages: 1) the landing page from the navigational link "eBay Sales Assistant"; 2) the page where the customer selects their data research package and inputs their data; 3) shopping cart; and 4) results page.

Finally, as you contemplate the database structure, I see the need for tracking of the following customer information: access to see their report; what they ordered; a short tracking of the survey results; and their contact information.
Buy Signed Copy of Maui CEO
Blogs—it seems like WordPress is hosting these now, I'm fine with that.

As noted earlier, I currently have the domain www.mauiceo.com through Domain Direct (domaindirect.com); you would work through them unless there is a reason to move the domain elsewhere, which I'm open to. I just want everything to work seamlessly.

Thank you again for your consideration. If you have any questions, please feel free to contact me via Skype.... <end>

If you need an administrative interface, outline the information that you would need to have access to and what will require updating. The developer can then help you determine if an off-line process is needed. Let me explain: if you want to update your inventory, you can either have a web page created where you manually enter the inventory information, or you can have the inventory updated from a database in your office. Other alternatives, such as acquiring inventory information from other web sources using web services, can also be implemented.

Outline the Data Requirements

In your requirements document to the developer, list all data that a) you want your application to keep just for further processing, and b) what data needs to be stored permanently. If you are accepting confidential information from an online user, such as credit card numbers, specify the level of security that is required. Most applications can easily be setup to use a secure channel between the web server and web browser using a technology known as Secure Socket Layer (SSL). However, if you are going to store credit card information in a database—which I discourage—you may want additional protection at that level. Keep in mind that you may be required by law or statute to notify cardholders if their personal information is accidentally released, or if obtained by non-authorized individuals.

Require a Mainstream Programming Language

You will most likely need to hire someone other than the original developer to do maintenance for you down the road. To ensure that you have the widest possible selection of developers, insist that the original site be built using one of the more common languages such as ASP.NET[67], ColdFusion[68] or PHP[69]. This language choice will also have an impact on the type of platform that the application will run on. For example, if you

---

67. ASP.NET is from Microsoft Corporation. See www.asp.net
68. ColdFusion is from Macromedia. See www.macromedia.com
69. PHP is from The PHP Group, and is a general-purpose scripting language that some feel is especially well-suited for Web development. See www.php.net

choose ASP.NET, you will be hosting it on a Windows Server. If you want to use a Linux or UNIX server, you need to make sure that the server supports the language your developer is going to use.

The choice of language also affects portability. As I mentioned earlier, if you use an outside hosting company like Domain Direct, you want to be able to transfer your web site from one hosting company to another if problems arise. Choose a language and platform that is prevalent in the industry. If you choose ColdFusion, your hosting company will have to have a ColdFusion Server and it will have to match the version of Cold Fusion that your site is built in. This can limit your options.

Choose an Appropriate Database

If your web site is small and not expected to get much traffic, you can use a database such as Microsoft Access to hold the data. This makes it easy to have information offline so you can analyze it using the query and report features of Access and you can even update your web site by just pushing the database via File Transfer Protocol (FTP) to the web host. More active sites will need more robust databases such as Microsoft SQL Server. There are a number of alternatives, and some are even free. Your software developer can help you decide on what is appropriate for your specific needs.

Choose a Developer Who Has the Appropriate Experience

If you fly on United Airlines, you can be assured that the pilot has a license and is trained to fly that type of aircraft. She is probably pretty good at the job. Contrast this with software development. In my experience, most of the people developing software are not good at it and don't have the education or training in order to do a good job. Unless you can interview and scrutinize a developer by making them write, interpret, or discuss code in great detail, you will have to rely on the word of others. The intricacies of web development, security, data access, and other aspects of the work require some good talent. Look at one of the developer's previous web sites will help you to see if the developer understands good page layout and workflow. Ask, of course, which parts of the website were their sole or shared responsibility.

If you use a site such as www.rentacoder.com, evaluate the developer ratings. Look over the developer's resume, and evaluate what kind of background they have. At time of writing, RentACoder has a section called "Top Coders," which lists developers who have completed lots of successful projects. Elance and Guru have similar rating systems, and even show how much money the developer/coder has made through their site!

In my experience, the best developers have degrees in Computer Science, Engineering, or Math. Business schools have Information Systems (IS) programs and many developers come from IS backgrounds. Virtually none of the IS developers have the skills necessary to write good code, because these B-school IS programs focus on spreadsheets and presentations, as opposed to a rigorous and demanding program that will produce good coders.

Since you're not looking to hire a junior developer but someone who can step right in and do the work, make sure the person has at least a year of experience doing specifically what is required for your project. If your project requires a team of developers, make sure the team leader has extensive knowledge and will review and approve all code developed by team members.

Site Hosting

The possibilities are nearly endless in the choice for a site hosting company. Based on your choice in Chapter 4 for URL acquisition, you may want to stick with the same company.

My previous recommendation was www.domaindirect.com, as I have used them for years. Recently, email performance has had glitches and performance has been slow. This is not acceptable in today's day and age, so I now recommend that you look at http://www.top10webhosting.com/ to get some other ideas. GoDaddy gets pretty good press.

Regardless of whom you select to do your site hosting, here's the reminder: make sure the site hosting company supports your database type. For instance, not all site hosting companies support Macromedia's ColdFusion, a wonderful web application development tool.

XML

XML, or Extensible Markup Language, is a markup language for documents containing structured information. XML is a new approach that has caught on with many programmers. From a business standpoint, XML allows you a structured way to tap into someone else's inventory and show that inventory as your own.

For instance, XML is evident on one of my favorite websites, www.ebags.com.

eBags offers a huge inventory, so many choices that I believe they do not stock the entire product line themselves. For instance, a review of their Top 10 bestselling laptop bags shows six bags which "leave [the] warehouse within 1 business day," and the other four bags "leave [the] warehouse within 2 business days." Since eBags does not know where I am (since I have not entered my zip code or other identifying information), the only reasonable explanation is that eBags will stock certain items in their own warehouse (1 business day processing), and "drop-ship" all other bags from other suppliers' warehouses (2 business day processing). XML is the means by which eBags ties into other databases and inventory systems—thereby allowing eBags to show inventory as their own.

For those of who want to utilize XML to the fullest extent, visit www.doba.com. Doba allows you to list some or all of their inventory on your website ... and these retail merchants will drop-ship directly to the buyer. Cool. I'm not sure how profitable, but very cool.

Merchant Integration

As mentioned earlier but repeated here, you have three easy options to process credit card payments: a) Verisign; b) PayPal or equivalent; and c) Escrow.com.

Verisign is the leading company which enables your online business to accept all forms of payment, such as credit and debit cards, and checks. See www.verisign.com. Using templates available from Verisign, your business will:

- create a script (called a "Gateway") to interact with Verisign;
- send customer information to Verisign (thereby requiring purchasers to enter personal information only once);
- process the credit card charge; and
- return an approval or declined key.

There is a nominal charge to use Verisign; however, you do need to have a merchant account, and I described the need for a merchant account (and how to get good rates) in Chapter 4.

The alternative to Verisign is to use pre-designed gateways between your site and either PayPal or Escrow.com. PayPal and Escrow have similar functionality to the Verisign setup I described above. PayPal and Escrow are easier to install than the Verisign gateway. Further, PayPal has *de facto* integration with eBay, and is probably the way to go for your business. See www.paypal.com and www.escrow.com. Online escrow, and a proposed way to have escrow for all of your transactions, were described earlier in this chapter. Don't forget: if escrow is your default, why do you need two gateways? Answer: Escrow.com and Paypal.com.

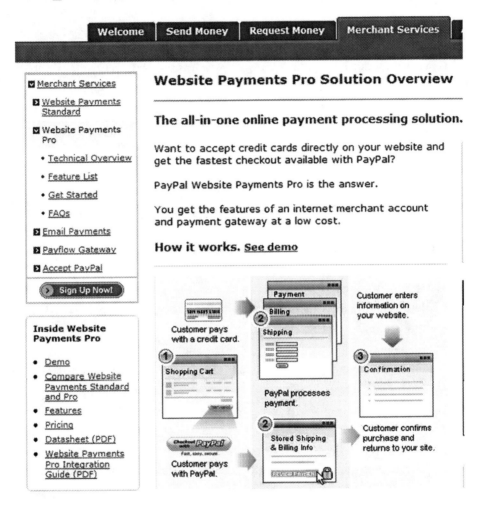

PayPal

Sign Up | Log I

Welcome | Send Money | Request Money | **Merchant Services**

☑ Merchant Services
▶ Website Payments Standard
☑ Website Payments Pro
  • Technical Overview
  • Feature List
  • Get Started
  • FAQs
▶ Email Payments
▶ Payflow Gateway
▶ Accept PayPal

Sign Up Now!

Inside Website Payments Pro

• Demo
• Compare Website Payments Standard and Pro
• Features
• Pricing
• Datasheet (PDF)
• Website Payments Pro Integration Guide (PDF)

Website Payments Pro Solution Overview

The all-in-one online payment processing solution.

Want to accept credit cards directly on your website and get the fastest checkout available with PayPal?

PayPal Website Payments Pro is the answer.

You get the features of an internet merchant account and payment gateway at a low cost.

How it works. See demo

Customer pays with a credit card.

Payment
Billing
Shipping

Customer enters information on your website.

① Shopping Cart

PayPal processes payment.

② Stored Shipping & Billing Info

Customer pays with PayPal.

③ Confirmation

Customer confirms purchase and returns to your site.

You can integrate PayPal pretty easily into your website, with the simple buttons or a more complete solution like the "Pro" version above. What I like about PayPal is that they will always be well-integrated with eBay. Also, PayPal is at the forefront of fraud detection; for instance, they have increasingly sophisticated algorithms which monitor a large combination of factors in determining the risk of a certain payor—including combining knowledge of the customer from eBay transactions and feedback with the

PayPal-based transaction at hand. Google payments are also an option, but at time of writing, pose no serious challenge to PayPal for our purposes.

Getting Your Website Up

Once you have space available from your hosting company, files can be uploaded to that space. These files will include your database/shopping cart; your core navigation template and web pages created by your brand identity company; and any files needed for the site's integration with the merchant processing.

Over time, you will need a mostly automated process for updating the timeliness and freshness of content on your site.

For now, find a simple way to send and receive files. Of course, based on the choices you made earlier in this chapter, your method of sending and receiving files may be dictated for you. Also, your Elance developer may have included this capability in their bid, typically with Linux-based, limited functionality.

If you don't yet have this capability, consider IP Switch's FTP Professional software. This software, believe it or not, will be the channel through which you can run your business from Maui! The software's "Synchronize" utility keeps your remote sites up-to-date by automatically uploading files, which have changed, while deleting files that you've removed from the master directory. The scripting automates the transfer and management of files. While you're golfing in the afternoon, your FTP script uploads certain files at regularly scheduled times. There are free versions of FTP out there, but like I said, having robust file management capability to start will benefit your new lifestyle later. See www.ipswitch.com.

Summary

If this chapter seems too technical after your second or third time through the text, you have two options. First, you can just use a pre-canned shopping cart and database. Your site hosting company will have one. The biggest downside is that you are stuck with that program's limited functionality.

The second option is to take the information above, and have a bidder on Elance.com *write the technical specifications* for you. Then, you take those specifications and bid them out. For illustration, your bid request could say:

> "We want to build a web site that will offer Jacuzzis for sale. Having already developed the home page and navigation bar, we are looking for someone to fully develop the other website specifications. We will take these completed specifications and bid them out to developers—including your own team if applicable. The website will focus on showcasing a few products; should utilize a mainstream programming language such ASP.NET, ColdFusion or PHP; and meet our business needs. These needs, as well as our timeframe, are articulated in the attached file."

Once you have your specifications done, you're off to a great start. You have used your words and language to articulate the business needs; these needs are translated into technical specifications; and the specifications are translated into working code.

Now, let's figure out where to store those Jacuzzis!

8

Finding a Warehouse Distribution Center

What's the best place for a warehouse? Long Beach, California. What's the most important requirement for your warehouse? Read on.

As you setup your businesses' logistics, make this a goal: touch the product as few times as possible.

Ideally,

- Have your supplier pack the product in a way that your freight company can deliver. Depending on your product's dimensions, that usually means putting the product on a pallet. In contrast, your supplier will be focused on packing the maximum number of units in a container—because this is what everyone else wants.

- Try to get photos of your product before the items are packed into the container. This helps you pre-sell them and increase your turns ratio.

- The supplier will also wrap the product in a way to keep out the #1 ailment of international shipping—dust.

Speaking on the first bullet above, you can get the transport requirements from your freight company (like Yellow[70]), then impose those requirements on your Chinese supplier. Why not have your product put on pallets in China?

70. See www.myyellow.com

This will greatly reduce the chance of damage when the container is unloaded at your warehouse, for instance. Many warehouse accidents are forklifts driving their prongs into the product. This is prevented when the product is on a wooden pallet.

Additionally, consider having your supplier build a sturdier wooden crate around the product.

This will cost you a little more in China but a lot less in your home country[71].

Your Business Process

Here's what you want your business process to look like:

- Order a container-full of product
- Product is shipped from China to your U.S. warehouse
- Product is stored safely in the warehouse without being disturbed
- Product is sold online and delivered, via freight company, to the buyer

Based on this simple explanation of the process, the following describes what to look for in your warehouse company.

What To Look For In Your Warehouse Company

First, you do not own the warehouse, but rather lease space from a warehousing company. This gives you the most scalability if your business grows, and minimizes your downside if the business is a flop. Many warehouses have a minimum billable of $300 per month—an amount which is much less than what you would have to pay if the warehouse were of the more traditional type.

Additionally, you do not have to have employees staffing the warehouse! The third-party warehouse does all the work for you, including pulling that pool table off the rack and giving it to the freight company for delivery.

---

71. Returns can bring an online company to its knees. Standard business legend states that returns cost 3x the product shipping. I did a consulting project with a 125+ store drugstore chain, and discovered that product returns cost a disproportionate amount of retail employee time; were frequently not scanned back into inventory; oftentimes could not be returned to the manufacturer (products like cosmetics and vitamins); and invariably through off their inventory management system.

Second, you need the physical location of the warehouse to be cost-effectively close to your port of entry. This usually means that your warehouse should be close to either the Long Beach or Los Angles ports, if your product is coming from Asia; or in Florida, if your product is coming from Europe. Of course, a Southern California warehouse can serve both Asian and European shipments, but the European product must come through the Panama Canal or be "railed" across the continent—a bumpy ride, I'm told.

For these two reasons alone, I recommend leasing warehouse space in or near Long Beach, California. For instance, Carson is a local town popular for warehousing.

One Carson-based choice is Schafer Bros Logistics. I've been in their warehouse at least ten times, where everything from wave runners to beer is stored. Schafer Bros' focus is on relationship building, and they can get the job done for you. See www.schaferlogistics.com.

For those of you wanting a more technologically-oriented company, with a higher level of service, capability, and price, Megatrux appears to be the answer. With everything from electronic data interchange (EDI) support to online inventory tracking, the offerings appear to be attractive. See www.megatrux.com.

The Most Important Requirement for Your Warehouse

This is an easy one: asset tracking. It may seem inconceivable to the lay reader, but warehouses can "lose" a motorcycle, pallet of beer, or piano with surprising frequency. Warehouses of the kind we're discussing in this book have 100,000 or more square feet, and their ability to manage each asset accurately is your most important requirement.

For instance, let's say you sell caskets. A customer in Provo, Utah orders a casket on Tuesday, and then cancels the order Wednesday morning before the shipment has left the warehouse. The casket was more than likely moved from the storage area in the warehouse to the outbound loading area. This is the scenario you want to present to each warehouse you are evaluating:

- What is the process for your business to contact the warehouse to cancel the order?

- How long will the product stay near the outbound loading area? Based on my experience, this area is the site of most accidents and product damage.

- How quickly is the product returned to inventory (both physically and digitally)?

- What is the charge for this transaction?

By asking these questions, you will have insight into how well that company can keep track of your assets. Asset tracking aside, you might also consider the following:

- Will the warehouse let you set up a photo studio inside the warehouse, if required? How much would the monthly charge be for a 20' x 10' reserved photo space? (Note: taking photos in a warehouse is tricky because of the light conditions, which is why a photo facility might be necessary down the road.)

- Can warehouse staff take digital pictures of an item on request, and what is the process and charge for this service? For instance, a customer may want a photo of the TV connections on the side of the Jacuzzi. You're in Maui, remember? How else will you get a needed photo?

- Ask about the frequency of damage claims and the processes for claims.

- General security of the facility, and how you can get a repair done on your product. For instance, if your product is damaged in the container, you will process a claim with the insurance company—but you still need to get the product repaired by a local technician.

- How the facility manages dust.

- Can you be allowed to authorize a verbal order over the phone?

As a practical matter, you will be managing this business remotely. Despite the wide availability of internet cafes and RIM blackberry devices, you still will need, from time to time, the ability to manage your inventory with a verbal request. Set up verbal authorization for moves now, with a simple password, and your life will be easier. Speaking of moves, let's move to the next chapter, which deals specifically with getting product from the warehouse to the customer.

9

Getting Product from the Warehouse to the Customer

After your container has arrived and been unloaded, what is your next action? We discuss your logistical choices, using technology to optimize the processes, and the importance of aligning customer expectations to logical reality.

At the 2007 eBay Developer's Conference in Boston, the following data was presented[72]. When buyers were asked "What one thing would you suggest eBay focus on," look at what was number one:

Solving the shipping concerns, and not over-pricing for shipping, will take you a long way.

After your container has arrived and been unloaded, now what? Sell a product, of course!

Once the order is confirmed:

1. Figure out which carrier is going to transport the item

2. Place the order with that carrier

3. Send a "release from inventory" order to your warehouse

---

72. "Lessons from eBay Buyer Research," Jeff Resnick of eBay, at the 2007 eBay Developer's Conference (Boston)

4. Inform the customer when they should expect delivery, and

5. Inform the customer on how to track the product en route.

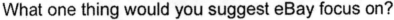

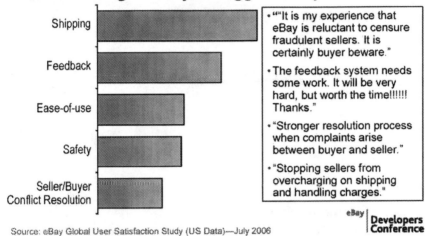

Buyers Want an Improved User Experience

What one thing would you suggest eBay focus on?

Shipping
Feedback
Ease-of-use
Safety
Seller/Buyer Conflict Resolution

- "'It is my experience that eBay is reluctant to censure fraudulent sellers. It is certainly buyer beware."

- The feedback system needs some work. It will be very hard, but will be worth the time!!!!!! Thanks."

- "Stronger resolution process when complaints arise between buyer and seller."

- "Stopping sellers from overcharging on shipping and handling charges."

Source: eBay Global User Satisfaction Study (US Data)—July 2006

eBay Developers Conference

Selecting The Carrier

You cannot use UPS or FedEx Express (which is different than FedEx Freight). Great! That's the point. As I mentioned earlier, because your product exceeds these carriers' weight and/or size restrictions, you have a barrier to entry which keeps out some of your competition—at least for now.

In selecting the carrier, I recommend that you set up business accounts with both FedEx Freight and either Yellow or similar trucking/freight company. By setting up accounts, you can get discounts and set up a nice, easy process for your employees to follow.

You should ask for a 52% discount off of the shipper's rack rates. No kidding! If they won't give this discount to you, look for help through an industry organization. Mentioned earlier in the context of getting a merchant account, industry organizations such as the National Association of Music Merchants[73] have pre-negotiated shipping discounts with freight companies.

UPS Quick 31% Savings

For a quick 31% off UPS for packages processed on eBay, see www. savewithups.com/ebay.

FreightQuote—Shipping Arbitrage

A viable alternative is to outsource each quote, in order to get the best possible rate. I shipped 300 lbs of speakers once using www.freightquote.com, and had a good experience.

The process is pretty simple: enter the pickup and delivery information, product details, and then you are given a few options to choose from. The options include vendors you may have a preference for or against, but also different delivery timeframes, insurance coverages, and so on. I like the homogeneous features of www.freightquote.com, www. highwayfreight.com, and www.integres.com. Finally, make sure you check out www.redroller.com, which claims to be fully integrated with eBay. This is a dog-eat-dog business, so the market leader today can be gone tomorrow.

---

73. See www.namm.com

Placing the Order with the Carrier

Most carriers still like faxes. In order for you to fax in your shipment order from Maui, you need either a standard fax or multi-function device—or remote fax capability from your PC. Therefore, I highly recommend eFax. You can convert most any file type (like Microsoft Word) into a fax and send that fax remotely. You can also receive faxes directly into your e-mail inbox—another prerequisite to working remotely. eFax also lets you choose between a toll-free fax number and a specific area code. If you want a Las Vegas area code, eFax can get you a fax number starting with the 702 area code. In fact, if you're selling cases of Chilean wine, you can even get the appropriate international fax number! Good for certain cases of company branding, the faxes are still routed to your inbox—wherever you are.

See www.efax.com and order the Messenger Plus service—a deal at less than $20 per month.

When you place the order with the carrier, make sure you have the appropriate insurance amount. Also, you **must** indicate that the delivery requires lift-gate service. The lift-gate is a ramp at the back of the truck that can be raised during unloading and loading. Tell your freight company whether you need lift-gate service at the customer destination only or at your warehouse as well. Lift-gate service tends to cost about $50 on each end. These big trucks are going to pull-up in front of the house or apartment and unload the container in the driveway, garage, or parking lot—and the customer is not usually equipped to unload something heavy out of the back of a tall truck. It is the customer's responsibility to deal with the product from that point. To better illustrate what this looks like, see the following:

These photos illustrate the process as seen by the customer.

Send a Release from Inventory

Your warehouse vendor is not going to release your product without proper authorization. This authorization generally takes the form of a fax from you or your authorized representative. Each warehouse has its own format requirements for the release, but you will generally say something like the following:

"Please release inventory item # 123456, serial # abc789, from our inventory. FedEx Freight has confirmed pickup for the morning of 02/23/05. FedEx Freight will have lift-gate service, but may require assistance. If you have any questions, please contact Victoria Smith at 714.555.1212."

Set the Customer Expectations First, Then Inform Them of Status

You are not shipping a FedEx Express envelope that gets there by 10:30 a.m. next day. But this is the very expectation secretly had by many buyers. The reality is that freight companies, and particularly carriers dedicated to a segment (like specialized piano movers), have challenges meeting their delivery commitments. These challenges are not typically within your sphere of control.

Based on these challenges, consider setting the customer expectations a certain way—then exceed that expectation. By analogy, imagine a flight from Chicago to New York that leaves at 9:00 a.m. and arrives at 12:04 p.m.

Northwest Airlines may show the official arrival time at 12:04 p.m., for instance, but knows from thousands of flights that the actual arrival time will be around 11:42 a.m., assuming that the flight left Chicago on-time. Bingo! Since many flights do not leave on time, Northwest has padded their expectation. If the flight leaves 15 minutes late, the plane can still actually arrive in New York *early*—according to the commitment and customer expectation!

In our case, if the data from the carrier suggests a Thursday delivery, tell the customer delivery will be on Friday. Or, depending on your product, you can pad the delivery schedule even more. One idea is for you to get the expected delivery date from the freight company, say Thursday; and then tell the customer that the product will arrive on Monday (confirming customer's availability).

Then, tell the freight company to hold delivery until Monday. There is usually not a charge for this short hold period. Once done, you are accounting for inevitable delays on the warehouse to freight company baton pass.

Of course, customers today are expecting tracking numbers, so you need to pass this information on to the customer. If using escrow, the tracking number is also required by the escrow company.

International Shipping

International shipping can certainly be done, and the process seems to get easier every day. If you feel up to the challenge, I can help you. First, let's make this clarification: Early on in your business life, you can ship internationally; but you still are targeting U.S. customers. After you have built up some profits and experience, then you can start targeting non-U.S. customers. I know one online seller who has done just that—he focuses on France now as his target country.

Getting a large item shipped to a destination outside the U.S. 48 states is not as difficult as you might think. First, read the following suggested text for your international shipping policy:

> International shipping is also available. For all destinations outside the 48 contiguous United States, we first crate your item in our Los Angeles warehouse for extra protection (crating fees are included in the shipping quote) and your product is then shipped via common carrier. Common carriers will deliver the item to your home but will not bring the item inside of your home. In Alaska, Hawaii, and Canada, delivery arrangements can sometimes be made directly to your residence. Otherwise, the product is typically shipped to the customs broker nearest you. Because of the language barrier, it is more efficient for you to then arrange for the pickup and local delivery.

> Additional duties, taxes, and customs broker's fees may be applicable for destinations outside of the 48 contiguous United States. For example, most goods imported into Canada are subject to the Canadian Goods & Services Tax (GST), which is currently at 6% and is calculated after any applicable customs duties are applied. Some Canadian Provinces also have a Provincial Sales Tax (PST), which varies by each Province. Other provinces such as, but not limited to, New Brunswick, Nova Scotia, Newfoundland, and Labrador have a flat Harmonized

Sales Tax (HST) of 15%, instead of paying the GST or the PST. For complete details on the applicable fees for your delivery area, please consult with your local customs regulation officials.

The common carrier (like Yellow or FedEx Freight) will deliver. The common carrier, with which you have an account, will typically outsource the foreign-soil delivery. The product will be delivered to the buyer's country border and taken through customs by the buyer's customs broker. Then, delivery will be completed to the customer's front door (but not usually inside the customer's home). Just like the "use taxes" for the United States, you need to push responsibility for taxes, duties, and so on to the customer.

By selling a few items internationally, you will build up valuable experience to apply later.

10

eBay, PayPal, Escrow, and Your Security

eBay will undoubtedly be one of your channels. I tell you how to minimize everyone's risk through escrow, spoof prophylactics, PayPal verification, and so on.

With the unbelievable market size and growth rate of new customers, eBay will be one of your important sales channels—if not the most important channel. In fact, it is arguable that your website should support your eBay sales—instead of the other way around!

eBay is the subject of many books—10,643 on Amazon, to be exact[74]. And there are hundreds of active categories. Here is an example:

As you can see in the graphic above, which is a screen shot of the newly redesigned home page, Categories are, in conjunction with a feature called "Related Keywords," a good way for buyers to find items if not using the classic Search.

---

74.   Why else do you think I have "eBay" in my book title? The number of book titles with "eBay" in the title was based on a search done July 2, 2007 at 8:12 p.m. See www.amazon.com.

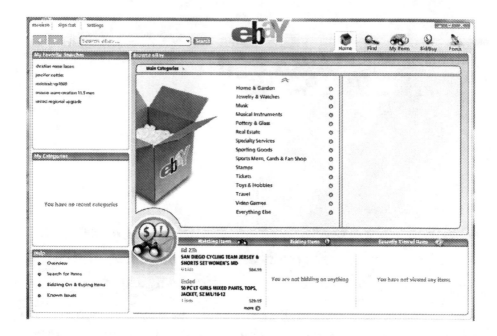

eBay Basics—Being an eBay Category Killer

There are lots of eBay books out there, and as we discussed in Chapter 1, Maui CEO is not intended to cover the daily mechanics of buying and selling; instead, you are provided a business and procedural framework that allows you to dominate your eBay category. To be an "eBay Category Killer" means to be the dominate seller in that category or subcategory. You are able to dominate because you have set up a low-price structure to be the low-price leader in the category. You offer reasonable customer service and reasonable product choices, but market-leading low prices. It is that simple.

Instead of covering the topic generally, here are my specific suggestions:

1. Outsource the development of your eBay selling format just as you did your website. Have the fonts, colors, logos, and structure match your website. The auction text must look professional.

2. Integrate interactivity and functionality into your auction text. For instance, have someone on eLance create a java script (or one that takes advantage of Adobe AIR, see below) that calculates shipping to each and every state.

3. Start your auctions out at $100, and sell with no reserve. Remember, no one can touch your cost. Selling with no reserve gets more bids on the auction, which raises the final sales price. Also, selling lots of expensive, big items bumps up both the number and credibility of your positive feedback score. Your goal is to be an eBay PowerSeller[75], because PowerSellers clearly get higher product margin.

4. Pay attention to the day and time of auction ending. Depending on the product you're selling, I believe that you could consistently get better action on certain days. When I ran my last business, I liked auctions to start and end at 11:00 a.m. PST, so that all primary U.S. time-zones were in play; everyone has ready access to the web at work or home; and buyers aren't busy picking up kids from school. However, as of October 2007, eBay's VP of Internet Marketing told me that, site-wide, mornings and evenings have higher ROI for Yahoo and Google paid search click-through's. I can tell you exactly the best time for your category on www.mauiceo.com.

eBay Data-Mining

Now, as a result of modern advances, we can analyze actual eBay sales data to give sellers empirically-based advice on auction data. Let's look at historical sales data on "grandfather clocks" between Apr 6 and July 4, 2007[76]. Here's just some of the information that is available:

---

75.   See http://pages.ebay.com/services/buyandsell/welcome.html.
76.   Search analyzed on July 8, 2007 at 2:12 p.m. PST with eBay.com data.

Total Sales:	$387,893	Total Listings:	1,503	Successful Listings:	504
Total Bids:	4,554	Items Offered:	13,205	Items Sold:	536
Bids per Listing:	3.03	Sell-Through:	33.53%	Sellers per Day:	12

Pretty neat, huh? Now, knowing the average sale price was $723.68 helps your knowledge of what's happening—and where you stand from a competitive standpoint. Let's look at what else I could provide you:

- *Featured Listing*: Paying eBay $19.95 to have your grandfather clock was a bad investment. In fact, **not one** of the grandfather clocks sold during this 90-day time-frame paid for either "Featured" or "Gallery Featured" options. I just saved you some money, right?

- *Multi-Listing*: Paying to have your item "multi-listed" was probably a bad investment as well. In this data set, of the 202 sellers who chose this option, only 78 auctions ended in a sale. This sell-through percentage of 38.61% is just barely higher than the category average of 33.53%. OK, I just saved you two listing fees and more! However, IF the data went the other way, namely, sales data seemed to justify the additional expense of multi-listing, I could tell you that the two categories with the highest sell-through percentage were Antiques (where you listed it originally) and Collectibles, where the sell-through percentage was a nice 69.91%.

- *Sell on eBay Stores or via eBay Auction?* As it turns out, only 12.35% of grandfather clocks sold through the eBay Store, but the lion's share of sales happened via Bid Auctions (84.74%). Buy It Now (11.21%) and Live Auctions (9.48%) weren't productive, but giving customers a second-chance offer was a winner at 100% redemption.

- *Auction Duration*: the eBay data-mining tells us that listing your grandfather clock for either five or seven days had about the same success (54%), but three day auctions increased the sell-through (61.33%) while ten-day auctions lessened your chances of success (26.79%).

- *Best day and time to have auctions close*: by crunching the data, in my category and with the product of choice, I can affirmatively tell you that your grandfather clock auctions should close on Sunday between 6:00-7:00 p.m. That is, holding all else constant, grandfather clocks had the highest sales success rate if they end within this time window.

Wow! If I only had this kind of data, well, my life would've been much easier. I actually had to pay two employees about three weeks of pay each to gather this kind of information manually (and then I still didn't have the granularity available now).

To see what kind of eBay data-mining is available, visit mauiceo.com, and click on the eBay Data Mining link. Our data license costs five-figures, not counting our evaluation, strategy and formatting time, so we have to charge for this service. However, for the first 100 buyers of this book, we provide a one-time discount of 50%. Enter promo code 91176.

What a summary could look like:

Recommended	Not Recommended	Neutral
Bold ($1.00)	Gallery Featured ($19.95)	Multi-Listing (2x)
Buy It Now ($0.25)	Home Page Featured ($39.95)	Reserve (1%)
Category Featured ($19.95)	Gallery ($0.35)	Subtitle ($0.50)
Gift Listing ($0.25)	Highlighted ($5.00)	
Picture Services ($1.00)	10-day duration ($0.40)	
Scheduled ($0.10)		

eBay Desktop, Otherwise Known as San Dimas—The New Interface

Success on eBay is based on a combination of factors, and like a river, is constantly flowing.

Note that at time of printing, eBay is changing their entire front-end interface. Called "San Dimas," the interface runs like a desktop application as opposed to a browser. San Dimas will provide a new search interface, different ways to bid, access to your personal eBay history, and so on. Written on top of a cool Adobe application, this will change your approach in the following ways:

- Watch your Google advertising spend very, very closely when eBay decides to launch this beyond the Beta testing period. Google and eBay really don't like each other, but depend on each other in many ways. For instance, it's rumored that eBay is the biggest paying advertiser on Google. San Dimas theoretically gives eBay more security (because it's not running in the oft-attacked browser), but I see ways that neither Google nor Microsoft's interests are furthered by San Dimas' success. So just watch your Google ad spending tightly at time of San Demas GA launch.

- Any automation software, whether in-house or in-market, might not work correctly.

- Look to take advantage of the new platform's capabilities—and circumnavigate or mitigate its weaknesses. For instance, the platform—called Adobe Integrated Runtime ("AIR"), enables very rich application development. When I saw a demo in June 2007, the platform really emphasized the visual. So, have your eLance developer do something cool and useful with it. There is a Software Development Kit already available, but of course if your developer didn't know this, use a different developer for this project. I mentioned weaknesses earlier, and since the final product hasn't been released, it's difficult for me to say exactly what the weakness will be. However, if this is good for buyers, it may not be good for sellers. For instance, if the application allows "competing" products to be shown on the same page, this may or may not be a benefit to you—haven't sellers already been cannibalized and commoditized enough?

Academics would characterize the majority of eBay auctions as a "B to C" model, or business to consumer. My brother calls eBay an "S to S" model, or shyster to sucker. As buyers have learned, fraud is rampant. There are at least three ways to protect yourself and business: escrow, spoof prophylactics, and verification. I will discuss each of these in turn.

Escrow

Online escrow is very similar to offline escrow. Buyers send money to a third-party (the escrow company), and receive undamaged merchandise before the seller is paid. For sellers, escrow can be considered as a cost of doing business, and theoretically helps protect sellers from credit card fraud.

Instead of explaining the process here, let me refer you to the current online market leader for this service: Escrow.com.

Once familiar with the details, let me give you a few suggestions:

- Make escrow part of every transaction, by default. This adds a connotation of security to your site and processes.

- Try to get customers to opt-out of the escrow by offering them a 5% discount in the checkout process. Escrow has a "time value of money" cost to you as the seller, and you'd rather get payment through an online bank wire anyway.

- If an escrow transaction is used, make sure outbound shipping is not refundable, and set up a reasonable charge for return shipping.

These terms are setup by you as account defaults with Escrow.com. Of course, if you worry about a customer for any reason, consider escrow. My experience shows, however, that from a legitimate seller's perspective, escrow heavily favors the buyer's interest.

Returns Policy

I talk about returns here because the use of escrow requires a well-defined return policy. Spend a couple hours thinking through your return policy. An old rule of thumb states that a return costs a business three times what was spent to ship the item. Since your Jacuzzi will cost $400 to ship, for instance, you can see that too many returns will quickly kill your business.

One idea is to require the buyer to pay half of outbound shipping in a return. For instance, if you charged them $500 for shipping the product from your warehouse to their door, the buyer would have to pay $250 to return the item. This policy balances the risk between the parties and provides some pre-purchase comfort to the buyer.

Spoofing

Spoofing is when someone pretends to be someone else. Spoofing is usually done through email. These emails may appear to be from legitimate companies that you do business with—such as your Citibank, eBay, PayPal, or your Internet service provider. You are often asked to validate or confirm your personal information by sending a reply, clicking on a link, or opening an attachment. Take it from someone who has been a victim of spoofing—and lost over $30,000—be aware!

How can you be alert to spoofing? By using spoof prophylactics, you can help protect your business.

First, tell customers that they will receive e-mail contact **only** from a certain e-mail account(s). In other words, on your home page and where also appropriate, you should say "Panda will only send you e-mail from 'info@panda.com' or 'status@panda.com.' Why bother? Spoofers will pretend to be you in order to get money from your customers or potential customers. A new tactic will be to create an e-mail account that looks like you, but of course is not you. For instance, the criminal mind will create an account called panda@hotmail.com, infopanda@aol.com, or anything that closely resembles your true e-mail account. Therefore, by clearly articulating exactly which e-mail account(s) customers will be contacted through, and only through that account, then you can help reduce spoofing.

Second, you should create a spoof verification e-mail account. This account should be formatted like spoof@[bizname.com]. If a client has any questions about the legitimacy of a communication from you, the client can send an inquiry to this account. Note that eBay uses an automated process now to respond to spoof inquiries. If your business has the need, installing an automated process to examine forwarded customer e-mails may be worth the license fee.

Third, your business needs to clearly articulate that you do not send or receive money through Western Union. Western Union is the most common channel used by villains spoofing legitimate businesses. I do not intend to demonize the company, but the verification process does not match today's on-line security needs.

Fourth, you should list **all** auctions as "private." eBay initially instituted private auctions to protect the identity of bidders in certain types of auctions (such as adult videos). This connotation has not carried on to the present, because many automobile sellers currently sell their cars in private auctions. Yet again, why bother? Because your bidders will be targets of fake emails. Someone will attempt to be you and collect money from unsuspecting bidders. Specifically, bad characters will send the second and third bidders from an unauthorized eBay "second chance offer," implying that the first bidder has backed out of the auction. By listing your auction as private, bidders identities are not visible to anyone but you the seller.

Fifth, download and install the eBay Toolbar. eBay Toolbar is a free add-in that gives you access to eBay from your desktop. Most importantly for our purposes, eBay has built-in spoof protection. According to the eBay website, the 'Account Guard' feature "warns you when you are on a potentially fraudulent (spoof) Website. It also lets you report such sites to eBay[77]." If anyone from eBay is listening, please don't bundle Yahoo (or anyone else) with the toolbar!

---

77.   www.ebay.com/ebay_toolbar

Finally, here's a plug for one of my former employers: if you're buying a new PC, consider one with either Intel® vPro™ (desktop) or Intel® Centrino Pro™ (notebook) processor technology. These PCs have hardware-based security features built-in, which are always more secure than software, and are sold by all the top PC OEMs.

Reporting Cyber-crimes

If you and/or any of your customers are subject to cyber crime, it should be reported to Internet Crime Complaint Center at www.nw3c.org. Almost anything is fair game, including theft of intellectual property rights, computer intrusion, economic espionage, online extortion, and money laundering.

Of course, fraud schemes such as identity theft, phishing, spam, reshipping, auction fraud, payment fraud, counterfeit goods, and even non-delivery of goods also are in their scope. The Internet Crime Complaint Center serves as a clearinghouse and repository of cyber crime complaints from private citizens and industry. They refer complaints to law enforcement agencies for investigation and prosecution. In 2006, these referrals resulted in almost 300 search warrants and 400 arrests[78].

Verification

I spoke with the Chief Information Security Officer from PayPal in June 2007, and he identified three areas they focus on: 1) brute-force attacks; 2) phishing; and 3) malware. PayPal has made good strides in dealing with the brute-force attacks, and about educating the public about phishing. Of these three categories, he was most worried about malware. Malware is software designed to infiltrate or damage a computer system without the owner's informed consent, which includes computer viruses, worms, Trojan horses, spy ware, dishonest ad ware, and other malicious and unwanted software[79]. Root-kit detection is critical to prevent malware, so when you

---

78.   See www.ic3.gov.
79.   As defined by Wikipedia on July 8, 2007.

update your anti-virus software, make sure you choose the version with "root-kit" protection.

There are several types of "verification" that you will come across, but let's focus on two: verifying you, and verifying the payer.

Verifying the Seller—You

eBay and PayPal have joined up to help verify your identify with a security key. This is basically a key-chain with a small LCD. Once synced with your eBay or PayPal accounts, it adds an extra layer of protection.

PayPal Security Key

This key makes an assumption: that your ID and password could already be compromised. That is, someone out there may already have these two items and could be waiting for the right moment to use them. So, drop everything right now and change your eBay and PayPal passwords—and make that a habit!

Use of the security key is free and the key itself is cheap—$5 at time of writing. After entering in your ID and password, the key generates a new six-digit code—which you enter on the website. You're in! Once used, a security key code expires. In this way, you now have yet another layer of security protection around identity verification.

Verifying the Buyer/Payer

eBay and PayPal have a verification process that helps authenticate identities. For instance,

- A person or organization registers with PayPal;
- PayPal makes two small deposits into the PayPal member's bank account;
- The member then completes the circle by identifying the exact deposit amounts.

This process means that the PayPal member has access to, and provided identification for, the legitimate bank account. Additionally, the member has registered a valid credit card.

Verification increases the trust of everyone involved. Your business should obviously become verified, a process available on the PayPal website. Additionally, if someone pays with PayPal, you should strongly consider a policy whereby you ship only to the verified address. I had a friend in grad school that shipped a Tag Heuer watch to Indonesia ... only to find that the PayPal payment was recaptured/rejected after the watch had already been shipped. This would have been avoided had he shipped only to the "verified PayPal address."

There are situations where legitimate buyers have genuine reasons for wanting to take delivery elsewhere. For illustration, a Dad may want to buy a pool table for his son at an out-of-state college. In this situation, I recommend taking payment by wire-transfer, or imposing a five business-day hold on PayPal funds before shipment.

Security and Outsourcing

Traditional businesses have financial and banking controls. These are for security as well as legal reasons. In our new world, here are some things to consider:

- Set up two-account systems when it makes sense. For instance, have two bank accounts, where all of your bank wires come into account #1, and then have "auto-sweep" enabled at the end of every day. This will sweep all funds into account #2, your primary account. When you provide customers your bank wiring instructions, don't give them your primary account information!

- Similar to the previous point, you should have two credit cards: one for you, and one for everyone else. I'll talk about outsourcing in a subsequent chapter, but you don't want to have your own *debit* card number provided to employees or, even worse, outsourcing firms in far-flung locales.

- **If you have someone primarily responsible for collecting payment or at least verifying that payment has come in ... give that person read-only access.** How you set up your labor strategy will determine your financial and banking control system. In other words, the strategy could be different if you have two employees sitting in your hometown versus outsourcing payroll to a local firm and email to India.

- Have a master password, if possible, and keep this to yourself.

It is now appropriate to talk about your labor strategy—organizational design, if you please—so let's move to that now.

11

Organizational Design

After your business starts to grow, what kind of employees and independent contractors should you hire? What about outsourcing to India or the Philippines? What is the best organizational design? Start with the goal of $200,000 of revenue per employee.

Your business is starting to make money. Now what? If you've read Timothy Ferriss' over-hyped *The 4-Hour Workweek*[80], the answer is "get out as fast as you can." I can't disagree more. 4-Hour Workweek spends a hundred pages talking about the author's exploits running around the world (without a laptop), enjoying the best excursions life has to offer. The book has a few gems, like getting someone in India with a heavy accent and unknown telephone number to keep calling your boss, or how the author won a fighting championship by pushing his opponent off the platform repeatedly (thus disqualifying his opponent through a rule loophole).

The commonality between *The 4-Hour Workweek* and *Maui CEO* is that both books preach that you can have a different life. The difference is that I am not the kind of person who is in the position or even wants to run from a business I just created the week before. We all want our jobs to be more than J-O-B-S, and we want more play time; our identities are often tied up in our work successes, and this is OK. Many of us are divorced,

---

80.   Timothy Ferriss *The 4-Hour Workweek* (Crown Publishing, 2007).

have kids in school, less-mobile family members, and friends and routines we actually enjoy in one location.

With that in mind, let's design your organization with flexibility and good decision-making processes. Ultimately, you might like to have yourself out of the business' day-to-day operations and available only for escalations—this allows you to move on and start another business. Sounds good to me.

The first inclination is to organize from a customer's perspective. I like the intention, especially if we were a customer-oriented business. We could divide the tasks/interfaces up between pre-sale and post-sale, and organize around those divisions. However, as I championed in Chapter 1, we want to have the *Discipline of Market Leaders*[81], and since our goal is to have little or no post-sale activities with a previous customer (other than positive word-of-mouth), this customer perspective-centric design just does not work for us.

We want an organization that is flexible, scalable if we grow quickly, and is low-cost where it makes sense. I give you the starting goal to have $200,000 of revenue for each employee. By employee, this means a person who is on your payroll as either a part-time or full-time employee. In the U.S., small businesses are often confronted with the choice: employee or independent contractor. If the person is an employee, you (the boss) direct their entire list of activities and tasks—you control their 40 hours completely. You also have the unpleasant pleasure of paying lots of taxes (primarily payroll), funding health insurance, providing meal periods and rest breaks, setting up a 401K, and so on.

As a result, small business employers tend to prefer having "independent contractors" instead of employees. If that person working for you is an

---

81. Michael Traecy and Fred Wiersma, *The Discipline of Market Leaders: Choose Your Customers, Narrow Your Focus, Dominate Your Market*, (Perseus Books Group, 1997).

"independent contractor," you don't have to pay for all the freebies and taxes; you just pay the person an hourly wage and let them deal with most of the paperwork (such as paying self-employment taxes). If you pay an independent contractor more than $600 per year, you do need to send them a 1099. I'm no employment lawyer, but as far as I know, the definitions and requirements (and how courts and administrative reviews have interpreted them) differ slightly between States[82].

Starting Point for Organizational Design (before outsourcing)

Here is how I organized a $1M *Maui CEO* business in 2002:

	Function	E or IC?	# Hrs Monthly	Location
John	CEO	E	180	NV / CA
Sheila	E-mail and customer first-line contact; logistics	E	180	SC
Nuray	Marketing, PR, Advertising, OEM private labeling	E	180	CA
Marissa	Admin support, collects and sorts mail, organizes bills for me to pay, and deposits any checks received; e-mail backup	E	120	CA
Jennie	Accounting / payroll interface, ROI on all activities, confirms sales posted matched deposits made, collections	E	40	CA
Jim	Web-site support, including changes, posting sales / promotions, customer data-mining, etc	IC	4-12	HA / MA
Payroll	Process the ridiculous number of payroll filings required, and manage our 401K plan	Out	varies	CA
Legal	Corp minutes; "scare" letters for the various jerks you occassionally encounter; board of directors' minutes; personal stuff like trusts	Out	$600 / yr	NV / CA
Accounting	Quarterly balance sheet and income statements; yearly financial statements and Fed / State taxes	Out	$1250 / yr	CA
Other	Business cards, marketing collateral, and so on	Out	varies	varies

---

82.   In California, the guiding statute is CA LABOR CODE SECTION 3350-3371. See also http://www.dir.ca.gov/dlse/FAQ_IndependentContractor.htm

Including myself, I had five employees, one independent contractor, and then outsourced the remaining functioned I needed. Let me outline my key learning from this design: I'll start at the top and work my way down.

- John: the CEO needs to guide the ship. You need to lead and be clear and concise in your instructions and assignments. Importantly, I learned to give each person below me exact guidelines on when they had authority to spend money or commit us. For instance, if we shipped an item to Kansas and the customer said it was scratched, Sheila was authorized to pay for local repairs up to $250, no questions asked.

- Sheila: the **most important** person is the one who answers email and is the first person your customer comes in contact with (whether via email or phone call or otherwise). This is your key hire. This person can live anywhere, and needs to sound like a competent angel on the phone. They will need to gain technical expertise around the product you're selling, but once they get in the swing of it, WOW, this thing really works.

- Nuray: I found that, as CEO, I wanted to be in charge of the marketing activities. Avoid PR firms; we spent somewhere north of $25,000 for the "best" small-business oriented PR firm we could find, and got virtually nothing out of it. Likewise, our advertising spend was almost entirely wasted; we found a huge positive ROI on Adwords, otherwise spending money sponsoring external events, advertising in magazines, and so on was a total waste. I also wanted to deal with our international OEM partners.

- Marissa: the administrative function is an interesting one: many of the routine administrative tasks (basically, running errands for the CEO) can be successfully outsourced to India or elsewhere. However, you cannot ask one employee to man the customer email account five days per week. They get too bored and annoyed; they also need a day to do "special projects" to keep them interested and feel like an import part of the org (since almost everyone else is working on various other "special projects"). So, I had my administrative assistant process email on Fridays and other times as backup to cover vacation days, etc. I just don't believe you can answer customer inquiries competently with an outsourced company. Things like logistics are more readily out-sourceable, and yes, and we will address those items soon. Also, the administrative assistant picks up the occasional check from customers who didn't use escrow or bank wire; waters the plants and feeds the dogs when you're traveling; and so on.

- Jennie: the financial analyst I had was excellent; she had an MBA and had worked in Finance at HP. This function can be out-sourced.

- Jim: web-site activities creep up on you, and this need is vastly underrated and under-estimated. This function too can be success-fully outsourced.

- Payroll: I used Paychex and they were able to handle all the payroll filings and having employees in multiple states. As implied earlier, one of the benefits of a corporate structure is benefits that accrue to you as the owner. One of those benefits was having an unusually high amount of contributions available through a profit-sharing plan—run and managed by the payroll entity. These contributions show up as expense items for your company (which reduces their taxable net income) … and you get a nice owner perk. Payroll can be outsourced on Elance; ask about their knowledge of tax-deferred retirement and profit sharing planning in our context.

- Legal: I would not outsource legal work, yet. Getting a nasty-gram from a law office half-way around the world does not inspire fear in the recipient. I actually think a 10-20 person firm is the right size to work with. Think about this from the person receiving the letter: if the stationary has 100 people's names on top, the recipient thinks "they're paying $350 per hour; I'll send a few letters back and forth and run up the bill—that's a victory in itself." In contrast, a letter received from a sole practitioner—who probably barely makes rent—also doesn't have the desired effect. The recipient probably thinks there's a lack of motivational firepower on the other end. Here are some cases I had to use legal help:

o Referral of the accountant: ask for the accountant who has been audited several times by the IRS, but never lost. That's your guy.

o Collections

o Inventory problem

o Activities mentioned already, like corporate minutes

- Accounting: as much as I would like to use Quickbooks, I used a genuine accounting firm to do the books. This helped me know that there was no fraud within the company. Also, if you ever wanted to sell your business (much less have an "equity event"), accounting documents from a reputable firm really legitimize your business.

- Other: things such as business cards, marketing collateral, and so on are certainly outsourcing candidates on the front end (design). I have some beautiful business cards I got in the Beijing suburbs, for instance. But with shipping, savings are negligible. So, have as much as you can out-sourced and then have a local printer (or whomever) finish the product.

Labor model—before and after outsourcing

Today is an exciting time where right-sourcing gets lots of news. Right-sourcing to me means balancing the lower cost of wages, usually because of global labor pools that are cheaper, against the pain in the ass it takes to have something done in said labor pool. I'm not trying to pick on Mr. 4-Hour Workweek, but seriously, certain things in our small business cannot be outsourced. I want to spend some time on India specifically in a minute. Let me now cut to the chase and tell you which functions I believe can be outsourced in a $1M *Maui CEO*-type of business.

Function	Original E or IC?	New E or IC?	# Hrs Monthly	Burdened US Labor	Right-Sourcing
CEO	E	E	180	$63	$63
E-mail customer front-line	E	E	160 (from 180)	$18	$18
Logistics	NA	Out	20-40	$18	$8
Marketing	E	Out	10 (from 180)	$34	$10
Local support for CEO	E	IC	120	$16	$13
ROI -- make sure you're making good financial decisions	E	Out	40	$22	$11
Web-master	IC	Out	4-12	$65	$10
Payroll	Out	Out	varies	$510 / mo	$2-510 / mo
Bad-guy	Out	Out	$600 / yr	$600	$600
Legitimizer	Out	Out	$1250 / yr	$1,250	$300-$1250
Business cards, marketing collateral, etc	Out	Out	varies	est. $3000	est. $1500
			Yearly Totals	$304,250	$208,440

As you can see from the chart above, I compare a well organized business from 2002 to an ideal structure for 2008 and beyond. I've been able to change the number of employees from five to two; the number of independent contractors (local) stays the same; and the rest is outsourced (locally or internationally). I'm assuming you the CEO are an employee, and talk about why in a future chapter (in summary: more benefits to you, including divorce protection). The phrase "burdened" labor rate refers to what you make per hour plus the approximate hit the company takes for benefits and taxes. The labor rate does not include these charges if the labor type is independent contract or outsourced.

Your e-mail person is so critical—and I mean the person with whom the customer interacts the most—I don't think you can outsource that to India. In my model, I've removed the logistics from that person's responsibilities and outsourced the logistics themselves. You open up an email account that says either tracking@[bizname.com] or status@[bizname.com] and these emails get automatically routed to your person in India.... who provides daily updates that are waiting for your e-mail person when they start their day.

I also think you realistically need your own local person for administrative tasks that you don't send to your virtual assistant. Some of these tasks are personal in nature where physical presence is required; watering your plants, picking up the occasional check from a customer, taking your kids to lessons or waiting for your car at the shop, and so on. Where physical presence is required, you need someone there. Since this isn't a full-time job and therefore you don't "direct" the person's entire work-day, you can make them an "independent contractor" and save lots of overhead.

I've tried to be conservative in my calculations, and based on my own experiences and what I actually paid people, today's networked economy allows for a $1M business to save about $100,000 in labor costs. I understand it's a flawed target for the purists, but you just went from $200,000 in revenue per employee to $500,000 in revenue per employee. You can throttle your own salary up or down to keep the company just barely breaking even (lower taxes). Finally, outsourcing allows you to not only reduce costs, but the opportunity to redesign many of your business processes to find both direct cost and productivity savings.

Pretty much everything else can be outsourced ... but to whom?

Outsourcing to India

India has a highly educated, English-speaking workforce. There are 500,000 engineering new graduates annually[83]. A financial analyst working in India would, in 2003, be paid $1,000 per month versus $7,000 per month or more to her counterpart in the U.S.[84] There are cracks in the armor. First, McKinsey & Co. estimated that just a quarter of India's computer engineers had the language proficiency, cultural fit and practical skills to work at multi-national companies[85]. As the "better" workers take jobs with big multi-nationals, you've got to wonder how good the solo virtual assistant is going to work for you.

Problems with India

I am worried about India for two additional reasons: escalating salaries and water. A July 2007 article in the Wall Street Journal says that small tech firms, who were leaders in sending work to be done by computer engineers in India, are now considering either bringing those jobs back to the U.S., or outsourcing to lower-cost locales[86]. Software engineers, whose U.S. wage inflation is under 3% according to Moody's Economy.com, are seeing their wages in India go up by 15%-50%.

Intel's own CEO is quoted as saying "the wage inflation rate for engineers in India is four times what it is here[87]" and I know from personal experience at Intel that employees in Intel will oftentimes leave for a better job—with their salary being tripled by the hiring company. There seems to be an emerging "endowment" affect—the rise in compensation gives parallel rise to the mindset that you must job-hop to get the raises that you deserve by endowment.

---

83.   Wall Street Journal Tues July 3, 2007 page A15
84.   Pete Engardio, Aaron Berstein, and Manjeet Kripalani, "The New Global Job Shift," *Business Week*, February 3, 2003, p. 50.
85.   Wall Street Journal Tues July 3, 2007 page A15
86.   Wall Street Journal Tues July 3, 2007 page A1 and A15
87.   Wall Street Journal Tues July 3, 2007 page A15

If wage inflation drives jobs out of India (as employers look for lower-cost labor pools), where will these jobs go? For high-tech, like web-site development, the most likely candidates (in order of low-cost to higher-cost) are Russia, Philippines, Malaysia, and China[88]. Parts of Mauiceo.com were designed by a company in Bangladesh, because I could get the work done there cheaper than India.

Finally, I am personally worried about how India's water problems will affect their future ability to provide sustainable services. This comment is a bit out of scope here, but inexpensive Japanese pumps have facilitated excessive aquifer drilling in India[89]. Simply put, India is consuming more water than comes in rainwater and the Himalayan glacier river-flows. With irregular monsoons; varying crop patterns and pollution; the political climate surrounding Himalayan water and Pakistan; and slow conversion of the population to urbanization, the shortfall in water is likely to be very acute and is likely to get worse over the next two decades. Water has become either saline, or contaminated with nasty things like iron and arsenic[90]. So, Indians pump water out of their back yards and fields faster than it is replenished, and the water table continues to drop. If this were China, water policy would be primarily national; India is in contrast a democracy and we see the economist's "tragedy of the commons"[91] being acted out.

Virtual Assistants

If you're just learning about virtual assistants (VA) from me, perhaps you should get out more. Hollywood stars have them, small businesses are starting to experiment with them, and there's even a Virtual Assistant Day (May 18).

---

88. See Chris Gaither, "US Workers See Hard Times," The Boston Globe, p. A10, November 3, 2003.
89. See *When the rivers run dry* (Beacon Press) by Fred Pearce (2006) pg. 35
90. See *Water Wars* (Riverhead Books) by Diane Raines Ward (2002)
91. Garrett Hardin, "The Tragedy of the Commons," *Science*, Vol. 162, No. 3859 (December 13, 1968), pp. 1243-1248.

I've mentioned Timothy Ferriss' *4 Hour Workweek* in less than glowing appreciation; his section on VA's is, however, an enjoyable read. Here's an example: his India-based virtual assistant is named Honey. Mr. Ferriss describes his task for Honey:

> "For some reason, the Colorado Tourism Board e-mails me all the time. (Most recently, they informed me about a festival in Colorado Springs featuring the world's most famous harlequin.) I request that Honey gently ask them to stop with the press releases. Here's what she sent:
>
> 'Dear All,
> [Ferriss] often receives mails from Colorado news, too often. They are definitely interesting topics. However, these topics are not suitable for "Esquire" [something he's working on]. Further, we do understand that you have taken a lot of initiatives working on these articles and sending it to us. We understand. Unfortunately, these articles and mails are too time-consuming to be read. Currently, these mails are not serving right purpose for both of us. Thus, we request to top sending these mails. We do not mean to demean your research work by this. We hope you understand too. Thanking you, Honey[92]'"

As I illustrated above in the organizational design section, you can save money by outsourcing certain administrative items to a competent VA like Honey. Since the VA's may move on to bigger and better things, you should hire a firm that manages VA's, instead of putting all your trust and training in one person—who can and probably will move on. The firm concept also manages payment collection and should have security processes in place to protect your personal and credit card information. These assurances would not be available if you utilize a one-person band—the VA's visiting uncle could steal your credit card number and then who has to deal with the hassles? You do.

---

92.   Timothy Ferriss. *The 4-Hour Workweek* (Crown Publishing, 2007), p. 116.

I'm going to recommend that if you have enough of the kind of tasks to support a VA, look in the Philippines first. Like India, English is spoken widely in the Philippines; however, having personally visited both countries multiple times, and having had a Filipino employee directly report to me, I find that I have a slight preference here. Back in December 2006, I outsourced exactly the same project to a team in both the Philippines and India. My cost was $225 in the Philippines and $400 in India. Both projects, once returned to me, had their strengths and weaknesses, but it did give me one strong data point.

In my opinion and experience, the person of Filipino-decent is slightly easier to understand over the vagaries of i.p. based telephony; is equally well-educated but has a more natural cultural fit with Americans on the phone; and is slightly less expensive. If you need charts and graphs, research or quantitative analysis, then India would be preferred. Alternatively, if you're looking for the classic VA-type activities, then post your eLance listing but limit it to the Philippines first, or keep it open worldwide but strongly consider my advice. If you travel to the Philippines, stay at the Shangri-La in Makati City (near the Manila airport); if you want to visit VA firms and actually hire one of them, you can setup payment via Chase Bank, which is very strong there, instead of paying with credit cards to save even more money.

12

Maui CEO Gets a Marketing Makeover

We address press relations versus advertising, and learn to apply multiple Harvard-type frameworks to evaluate and refine your offering—capturing pragmatists and their dollars. Positioning relative to your competition is also tackled.

By now, you've got a great website, your eBay feedback is going up, and you are sorely tempted to start advertising. What you should be doing, instead, is evaluating and refining your own offering instead.

Press Relations and Advertising

Let me deal with advertising and press relations ("PR") now. Since you're still a newbie, you should seek press first, which helps build your brand; advertising comes along later and helps reinforce that brand message. Let me save you $15,000 right now: don't hire a PR firm. I tried this and enjoyed meeting the good looking, really cool, and sometimes weird people that grace the halls of PR firms. However, the return on my investment was miniscule. Press is one way to legitimize your business. But press is also not as objective as you might think. The PR firm will help you focus the "so what?" message, which is harder than it sounds. I've dealt with the press in Asia (launching flash memory products in Hong Kong, Japan and Taiwan); in Europe (launching Intel's vPro™ business platform in Belgium, Great Britain and Germany); and in the US (with my small business). In all cases, you must be able to answer the "so what" question succinctly.

Like all activities in business, think about what success looks like: in this instance, success would be getting some TV and radio interviews (which lead to product sales), and getting your press article and/or "interview" picked up online—and written accurately. Then, when someone "Googles" you, they see the articles and your legitimacy is reinforced. Sounds like success, right? The problem is two-fold: one, there are no guarantees that your story will be picked up, even if your idea is cool, neat, and/or unique. This is my point above: despite what you want to believe, and what the PR firm will tell you, most of my readers would spend their money and getting little in return. The second problem, or rather opportunity, is that you can create legitimacy with or without a PR firm at the wheel. Use your testimonials properly, and you will start to establish yourself and/or business as experts in your field. Speaking at conferences, writing articles to the appropriate online journals, and membership in the right organizations can also bolster your early credibility.

My advice is to hire a freelancer to help prepare press kits and distribute your message; I see various packages for this service on Guru.com for $300 and up. I'll be reviewing additional options in the PR space and plan on providing up-to-date recommendations on the website; see www. mauiceo.com.

Evaluating and Refining Your Own Offering

I considered titling this section "Online Marketing," but resisted because the term is misleading. Online marketing implies that I'm going to tell you how to improve your banner ad click-through rate and tricks to make spam look like legitimate direct marketing. Instead, I want you to think of online marketing in this context: your website IS your marketing on the internet. Every good product has a trial period, and you've just completed your trial. We need to refine what you've got and will use the classic Marketing framework of the 4P's[93]—which is still very applicable to product businesses like ours. As usual, I'll use my own experience and put a practical application around the framework.

Promotion

This "P" of the 4P's typically includes various elements such as point-of-sale promotion, advertising and press relations. You will be able to have and manage your web-based point of sale promotions (like "best sellers" or "March madness"). You are still building your brand/image/reputation, so for now, most advertising is a waste of dollars (except pay-per-click search engine advertising, which I will cover later). And we just discussed PR. What is left? Word-of-mouth promotion.

I have put forth the idea that we don't focus too much on repeat business, because 1) low-cost leaders attract price shoppers who have little or no loyalty to the vendor; and 2) we're selling large items of which customers don't typically buy more than one. Because of these factors, you just can't change reality, and we have not built an infrastructure or too many processes that focus energy and resources on CRM (Customer Relationship Management) or post-sale programs. There is one very important exception: we need our happy buyer to tell others about us, namely word-of-mouth promotion.

Here's the challenge, as simple as I can make it: when discussing the great product and price paid, you (the seller) want the buyer to focus their sales-pitch on the pragmatic benefits while avoiding the revolutionary aspects of the purchase.

---

93. The 4 P's of Marketing help you determine the right "marketing mix" of products. The idea started in 1948 (according to Wikipedia) and was brought to market by Northwestern's marketing guru Philip Kotler. See Kotler, Philip, Keller, Lane (2005) "Marketing Management", Prentice Hall, ISBN 0131457578

Differences in People

Let me start this section with an example: a lawyer in Jackson Mississippi just bought a used Yamaha grand piano from you; you first had the piano shipped from your Los Angeles warehouse to a local factory, and had a brand new player system installed. (A player system accepts CDs and "plays" the music on the piano by having the keys move and hit the strings just as the original recording artist intended.) Finally, the piano is shipped from the factory to the customer's house, installed, and enjoyed immensely by the buyer. Now, consider all the people that will likely hear about or even see the piano—these are all potential customers. Which customer is most likely to buy from you?

- A fellow partner in the attorney's firm
- His sister
- His child's piano teacher
- His neighbor, a professional pianist
- His housekeeper
- One of his friends, when they see the piano while over for dinner
- A golfing buddy who always has the new Callaway driver

As you look at these potential customers, separate them into two categories: would you call them either an "early adopter," or "pragmatist"? These terms, and this concept, come from Geoffey Moore, a popular business author[94]. Let's define "early adopter" as the kind of person who can easily program complicated devices like the new espresso machine; is the person you call when you have computer problems; and is the first to get the Apple iPhone.

---

94.   Geoffrey A Moore is a managing partner at TCG Advisors in San Mateo, California, and venture partner at Mohr Davidow Ventures in Menlo Park, California. He is the author of the bestsellers *Crossing the Chasm, Inside the Tornado, The Gorilla Game,* and *Living on the Fault Line.* If you do nothing else, read Chapter 2 of *Inside the Tornado.* I personally heard a professor of business at Harvard University say "everything I ever did wrong in my career can be found in chapter 2" [of *Inside the Tornado*].

Contrast these personality types with the "pragmatist," who is in many ways the opposite of the early adopter just described. The pragmatist lets others work out the problems first; the pragmatist buys a cell phone that has a good connection above all else—they don't need all those fancy features. Pragmatists are price-sensitive, conservative, and skeptical. Without knowing our lawyer's friends and acquaintances firsthand requires us to take a guess as to where to place them on our chart. Go ahead and give it a try before you look. Early adopter or pragmatist?

Here is where I might place them:

Potential Customer	Early Adopter	Pragmatist
A fellow partner in his law firm		X
His sister		X
His child's piano teacher		X
His neighbor, a professional pianist		X
His housekeeper		X
One of his dinner friends	X	
Golfing buddy	X	

Again, these initial guesses are just educated speculation. I know that attorneys are typically conservative; hey, they still use WordPerfect and have administrative assistants do their typing! I'm also tagging our attorney's sister and housekeeper as pragmatists, along with the teacher and professional pianist. How many professional pianists, for illustration, would buy a piano sight unseen? Not many, hence the pragmatist classification.

Now, think about the first two natural responses our lawyer has when one of these potential customers says "Wow, I didn't know you got a new piano!" He would either say:

"I saved $8,000 by buying it online!" or

"Let me show you how these new player systems work!"

The early adopters are going to love our attorney's second response: the early adopter-types enjoy seeing the new technology and will connect with the message—the "word-of-mouth" message. This is a good start.

How will pragmatists respond to the lawyer's response "Let me show you how these new player systems work?" Pragmatists are probably thinking, "This guy has more money than sense—why didn't he just buy a Steinway? Who needs a piano that plays itself? That defeats the purpose." Pragmatists are practical, to be sure; and a *Maui CEO* business proposition will naturally connect with the pragmatist's frugality; low-price can help overcome some of the deepest fears a pragmatist might have buying something like a piano online.

Crossing the Chasm to a Pragmatist and Their Dollars

There are two things about the psyche of a pragmatist that, once known, can help you increase sales to this customer segment. First, pragmatist's value opinions from people they trust—people who are like them in terms of technology adoption. A fifty-five year female VP of Sales would value someone's opinion on a product much more if that other person was from Rotary or the local professional women's association; in contrast, the same woman is not likely to trust her daughter's friend studying environmental science at Berkeley.

The difference isn't necessarily about age, although age can contribute to creating one's philosophical approach around and experience with technology adoption. From a technology adoption perspective, Grandma doesn't relate to the young whippersnapper; the proud owner of a Ducati motorcycle (high-end, high-technology, and quirky) would not be too influential on a Harley Davidson owner. If you want to reach the pragmatist and their dollars, give them an opinion from someone they trust—another pragmatist—and not an opinion from someone who is utterly unlike them.

The second characteristic to know about pragmatists is how much they value the market leader. A pragmatist will buy a Honda for the good repair history, low cost of total ownership, and so on. They know that if the Honda dealer charges them too much for service, there will be lots of places in town that can service a Honda. Pragmatists stay with the herd. Pragmatists consult with their colleagues; in contrast, early adopters follow their own hearts.

This, then, is the challenge: how can you get your early adopter customer to "cross the chasm" verbally and connect with the pragmatist? Answer: in your post-sale communication with the customer, reinforce the pragmatic aspects of the purchase, and offer incentive for referrals. In our illustration above, let's see what we could say against common and underlying values of the pragmatist:

Underlying Pragmatist Value	You Could Reach By Reinforcing...
Analytic	Saved 45% off local store
Conformist	Has Renner hammers, like Top 5 pianos
Consult with colleagues	Popular with teachers
Manage risks	Money-back guarantee (less shipping)
Motivated by present problems	Study shows kids demotivated by keyboards
Pursue what is probable	Buying pianos online is where market has moved
Stay with the herd	Testimonials
Support "evolution" (not "revolution")	Same technology honed over the years

You can reinforce these pragmatist values in post-sale communications, like emails informing the buyer of shipping status. At the bottom of said email, have the signature line reinforce your top two choices. You could send a postcard that emphasized the values and reminded of the referral bonus. Doing so will help you convert that skeptical pragmatist into dollars and an evangelist.

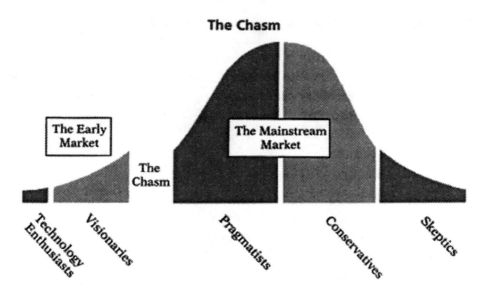

The Chasm

The Early Market

The Chasm

The Mainstream Market

The Chasm

Technology Enthusiasts

Visionaries

Pragmatists

Conservatives

Skeptics

Source: Geoffrey A. Moore, *Crossing the Chasm* (Collins, August 2002)

Now that you get the premise of what you can do to "cross the chasm," here is the actual graph used by Moore. For ease of instruction, I had simplified the segments. As you can see, the size of the market on the right side of the chasm is huge and critical. (This is a graph of the number of new customers.) We have thought about positioning in the context of psychology: differences in **people** and their adoption of technology. What about differences in **product**?

Product

Webvan spent more than $1B to create an online grocery business and was managed by top talent. But they went "kaboom!" The Segway was hyped like the Apple iPhone and even had Steve Jobs' backing, but has sold only 6,000 units in the 18 months after launch. Why have Webvan and Segway failed? Because they were able to capture the technology enthusiasts and visionaries (see chart above), but failed to cross the chasm to the pragmatists, followed by the conservatives, and so on. In addition to thinking about the chasm in terms of people, you need to consider differences in product.

Crossing the Chasm Slowed (or Prohibited) by Product Differences

If your eBay sales aren't up to your expectations ... or you are trying to grow your revenue, consider the following two points: businesses routinely underestimate the psychological costs of behavioral change; and buyers are irrational.

I tried Webvan once and enjoyed the convenience ... and then Webvan filed for bankruptcy liquidation. Listen to what their CEO Robert Swan said on the sad day: "Webvan has weathered numerous challenges, and in a different climate, I believe that our business model would prove successful ... At the end of the day, however, the clock has run out on us[95]." I disagree with the conclusion; in fact, the business model is still around and has been slow to "diffuse." Safeway has been selling groceries online since the Webvan days, for instance, but even techies like me aren't using the service yet.

Consider the advantages of buying your groceries from the comfort of your computer (or ultra-mobile PC or smart phone): avoiding crowds; convenience of online ordering; the service of having everything delivered; and how online ordering lets you match up your dietary goals (i.e. low-carb) with recipes and weekly planning. That's a pretty good list of advantages. How about disadvantages? From the executives' perspective, they saw the behavioral change as a small cost relative to the advantages. They were wrong.

Customers could no longer pick out the cut of meat they wanted; you get what the Safeway employee picks out for you. Customers no longer saw the in-store end-cap that reminded them to buy something they had inadvertently left off their list. I have no doubt that Webvan executives knew this. What they didn't count on was the psychology of gains and losses[96]. In 2002, the Nobel Prize was awarded for work that explored why individ-

---

95.   http://news.com.com/2100-1017-269594.html

uals stray from rational economic behavior. In other words, if the advantages outweigh the costs, why do customers still not bite? Two of the reasons cited include:

- Customers treat required behavior changes and shortcomings as large losses. These losses—like not being able to pick out your own Rib eye—have a bigger impact on a person's psyche than similarly sized gains.

- Customers weigh the options subjectively, not objectively. If the shipping charge is reasonable, hey, why not order groceries online? For instance, if customers weighed the $10 Safeway grocery shipping charge against the time value of money saved by not driving to the store, sauntering up and down the aisles, standing in line to pay, and loading up the heavy grocery bags ... they would see the objective value of online ordering. However, the perceived value, or should I say the perceived costs, of the things you lose when you change the status quo, are higher than an objective analysis would indicate.

I like this example from California: during the various power outages, customers demanded compensation from the local power company when a power outage occurred. To help balance the power grid during maximum use, the power company offers a year-round deduction to your electric bill if you allow the power company to throttle your air conditioner off when it's really hot and demand for electricity is highest. What's the difference between what customers demand in terms of compensation after a power outage—and what customers will pay to proactively avoid the problem? Three to four times as much[97]. This is because "losses loom larger than gains[98]."

96. "Eager Sellers and Stony Buyers," by John T. Gourville, Harvard Busines Review (June 2006)
97. "Eager Sellers and Stony Buyers," by John T. Gourville, Harvard Business Review (June 2006)
98. "Eager Sellers and Stony Buyers," quoting psychologists Daniel Kahneman and Amos Tversky, by John T. Gourville, Harvard Busines Review (June 2006)

I implied that Segway was also an example of where the psychology of change was underestimated. My first thought on Segway is actually a memory; I was in downtown Beijing, with the hustle and bustle, and saw a guy in a business suit go flying by on his Segway. As you can imagine, people were staring!

Rogers Five Factors of Diffusion

Let's put together the concepts from crossing the chasm and how losses loom larger than gains. What does the buyer get when they buy a Segway? Mobility. What do they lose? The health benefits of walking. Segway expected to sell around 75,000 units but only sold an estimated 6,000 units[99]. Had Segway been able to cross the chasm from enthusiast to pragmatist, and minimized the psychology of change, I believe their sales would have been much stronger.

Here's one more framework[100] you should apply to your product mix. It is believed by certain academics that 85% of your product's success is determined by the following five factors:

1. Relative Advantage—the degree to which your new product is better than what it replaces

2. Compatibility—is your new product compatible with the buyer's existing practices and beliefs?

3. Complexity—is the product easy to explain? Easy to use?

4. Observability—how "public" is the customer's use of the product?

5. Trialability—can your new product be experimented with on a trial basis?

---

99. "Eager Sellers and Stony Buyers," by John T. Gourville, Harvard Busines Review (June 2006) pg. 3.
100. Rogers, Everett M. (1995). "Diffusion of Innovations," Fourth Edition. New York, NY: Simon & Schuster.

Let's stick with Segway:

1. Relative Advantage—Segway is a new product category, but its relative advantage is low, because a new Yamaha scooter gets you there faster and is also environmentally friendly (both strengths of Segway relative to walking)

2. Compatibility—Segway is low here too; there are places to park and lock your bike, but where can you leave your $5,000 Segway outside the health club?

3. Complexity—Segway is a draw here: it's difficult to explain, but easy to drive; you just stand on it and lean forward

4. Observability—Segway scores high here. I will never forget that Beijing sighting of my first Segway. Assuming conspicuous (but environmentally-friendly) consumption is desired, observability is high

5. Trialability[101]—I'd rate this low as well; who knows where you kick the tires on one of these?

Consider your product line in light of these five factors. Remember that your product will sell more and sell faster if it rates higher in these criterion; success is defined as having low behavioral change required while creating clear value as perceived by the customer. After you consider your products against these conditions, you now know that you should emphasize your product's strengths and de-emphasize its weaknesses (or improve them).

Product Continued: Your Website

Your website IS your marketing message. You need to take a step back and look at your webpage as if seeing it for the first time—and with a critical eye. Is the visual presentation consistent? Is the content relevant?

---

101. Helio understands this concept, and offers to send you their brand new Ocean social-networking cell-phone for 30 days—for free.

Positioning Relative to Competition

Volvo stands for safety. If the Marketing department spent $50M attempting to change this positioning, the attempt would be ineffective; Volvo owns that little slice in your mind representing "safe cars." Because the positioning is so solid, relative to their competition, Ford, Mercedes, and Porsche can only be "safe as a Volvo." When we started *Maui* CEO, you were encouraged to be singularly clear on what product you sold, as a low price leader. Has there been scope-creep? Let's take a look.

Acting as if you were a customer, follow the process to get to the product website. Did you click on a paid link or search result? (Note this for later.) Was one value proposition more effective at catching your eye? For instance, would someone's offer of FREE catch your eye more easily than "best price"? Jump around, evaluate, and honestly narrow the choice down to two web-site sources. The results give you insight into your competition's strengths. Now, do the same thing on eBay.

Let me show you an example from actual eBay data. From April 13, 2007—July 11, 2007 (90 days), here are the top 5 sellers of doors:

Rank	ID	Total Sales	Total Listings	Successful Listings	Bids	Items Sold	Sold Price	Sell-Through %
#1	51368826	$37,785	109	21	23	23	$1,642.83	19.27%
#2	32403315	$28,754	31	31	31	31	$927.55	100.00%
#3	67462203	$13,888	89	3	3	3	$4,629.33	3.37%
#4	18141075	$13,405	7	6	6	6	$2,234.14	85.71%
#5	64223963	$12,786	6	5	5	5	$2,557.13	83.33%

Compare sellers #1, #3, and #5 (ranked by Total Sales) below: Grand Entrance Doors, Abby Door, and Lynda's Variety Treasure Box.

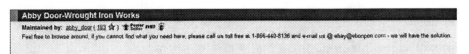

Grand Entrance Doors, the apparent leader, specializes in alder wood doors. Abby Door specializes in wrought iron. And Lynda's Variety Treasure Box specializes in mahogany doors. See a trend? Each is positioning themselves in relation to the wood of choice. This is a good start, although the business names do not lend themselves to be collaborative with the positioning (except for Abby Door—Wrought Iron Works). Each could do better by focusing more. A quick investigation shows that each company carries all kinds of things other than the doors (hinges, accessories). I'm certain that if you looked at these inventory items from an Activity-Based Costing angle, that you'd have a better return by selling only doors and not wasting your employees' time boxing up and sending door hinges.

Are you clearly differentiated from your competitor? If you are the mahogany door leader, then copycats face the uphill battle of trying to separate themselves from you. Not to mention the impossible task of underselling you, when you buy straight from the factory in Brazil, while the competitor buys from a distributor.

Technical review

Does your home page load quickly? Are the technologies used distracting? Do all the links work? This is stating the obvious but we've all been on websites—recently—where all three of these problems existed, and you moved on instead of waiting. Run http://webxact.watchfire.com/ on your site to give you feedback on your site's accessibility, content and privacy compliance.

Interactivity (tension on every page)

One of the qualities of a great writer (fiction or non-fiction) is having tension on every page. This is the pure definition of a "page-turner" and gives us a good standard by which to base our website's interactivity. Since it's believed that 80 percent of people read only 20 percent of a web page, and don't like to scroll down web pages, look at your page's density: break up your content into small pieces without destroying the flow.

One of my recent observations is that websites have information overload in their quest to be interactive. Give your visitors the information they have requested and naught more.

Motivation of Others to Recommend You

Many of the fun cases studied in business schools across America involve channel conflict and motivation. Inevitably, Sales is running on a different track than product management, which of course is in conflict with the ecosystem partners. One of my favorite cases is Aqualisa[102], where Aqualisa the company invented the best shower-head in a decade; priced the

---

102. Aqualisa Quartz: Simply a Better Shower (Harvard Business School Publishing), 2002.

product so that the retail establishment made more money than previous products; and saved the plumbers 75% in installation time.

There was one little problem: the plumbers didn't want to save installation time! It turns out that legal regulation in the UK basically requires new plumbing work (which this and most showerheads require) to be done by a certified plumber—and there was a six-month waiting list. Since these plumbers got a fixed price for installation, and demand for their time was high, they were disincentivized to promote the new Aqualisa heads. (To be clear, the plumbers believed that they would quickly catch-up on the back-log, thus ending their vital position in the cog.)

Since you probably don't have a sales force (although this isn't a bad idea—if VA's can competently act in this capacity), **run through each player in your supply chain** and assess their motivation to recommend you and/or help you sell product. You might find misalignment to repair and incentives to leverage.

13

Advertising in the Networked Economy—Google and YouTube, Paid Search and Viral Videos

We focus on search engine optimization and paid search. What's the area where you can get significant leverage, given your higher ASPs? Read on.

Based on my experience, most advertising does not work. I put product in fancy restaurants and furniture malls; advertised in trade-specific magazines; had prominent position at a trade show; hired a PR firm; and sponsored a competition. Virtually every dollar spent on these activities was wasted, and I'm not sure that even one sale resulted from the effort and time.

There are two areas of advertising worth your money—that is, there will be a positive ROI—and they include paid search and search engine optimization. Note how all roads lead to Rome, namely your website. Now, having that custom-built, snappy website will come in handy.

Paid search

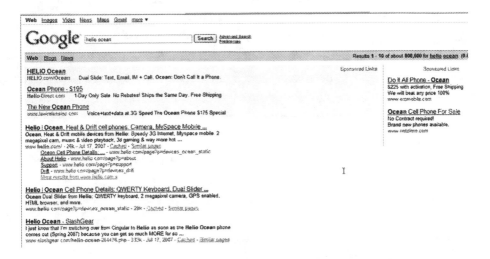

Paid search is simply what it implies: when someone types "helio ocean" in the search box, Google delivers three sets of data: Sponsored Links (i.e. paid search) at the top and also on the right side and free results below the yellow box. Those free results are theoretically based on how useful and applicable the websites are to the specific search terms. The higher up the screen you place in these free search results, the better. Coming up number one in the free search results is like getting a minute free commercial in the Super Bowl, and an entire industry has sprung up to support that goal. We will discuss how to improve your position on the free results page—otherwise known as search engine optimization—in the next section.

I'm kind of lucky today, because on the day that I am writing this section, someone is doing exactly what I think you should do in terms of paid search. Do you see the second result in the yellow box area—the "Ocean Phone—$195" ad? This ad caught my attention immediately, since I know that the phone costs $295 direct from the manufacturer. So I know that's a good price. It's "one day only," so there is a time element of urgency. The low price is clearly evident, because it's in large text.

I honestly looked at this page a few times before I even noticed that the third ad just below actually has a lower price ... but the price is lost in the "voice+text+data 3G" mumbo jumbo. Finally, when you do this kind of advertising, you can really focus your marketing dollars. You do a short-term promotion, and you can pay the big dollars to come up high in the paid searches ... but the big dollars can be spent for a short amount of time—as little as one day. Clicking on the paid search link takes you to the website, which is in a good position to make the sale.

Let's take a step back and start off at the 60,000 foot level outlining the "paid search" process.

- The segment is called "contextual advertising." Advertisers want to promote their products and services, but instead of the "shotgun approach" like a highway billboard, contextual advertising uses context (i.e. what you type on your smart-phone or computer) to serve an ad related and relevant

- When this ad is delivered, there is no charge unless the customer actually clicks on the ad. This model is referred to as pay per click (PPC) or cost per click (CPC). It can cost you, the advertiser, anywhere between 1 cent and 5 dollars for that click that brings the person to either our homepage or eBay store.

- Paid search, if done correctly, is absolutely worth your money. Over a period of two years (2002-2004), we were able to directly attribute $14 of revenue to a $1 ad spend on Google. Results vary based on a zillion factors, but I highlight key points in a minute.

- Google and Yahoo are the two leaders in paid search and are where you must start.

Google Adwords

Based out of Ann Arbor, Michigan, Google's program allowing you to buy paid search space is called Adwords. To explore Adwords, go to Google.com and click on Advertising Programs. Watch the demo.

The key to success with paid search is, obviously, buying the right keywords. Common words cost more money, while more obscure words cost less money. Certain keywords will be obvious for you based on your business. If you sell pinball machines, you would obviously explore "pinball" and "pinball machines." It turns out that both were fairly expensive to buy Top 3 placement (around $0.70 per click on "pinball machines" and $0.55 per click on "pinball"), but that just the word "pinball" had much more success than "pinball machines." It also turns out that both "pinball machine adams family" and "playboy pinball machine" were really inexpensive buys ($0.05-$0.40 per click), but had substantial traffic. The $0.40 can drop to $0.06 per click if you don't mind coming up in position 4-6 or 7-10. It's dynamic, meaning the price can change.

Google has a keyword suggestion tool, and this is a good place to start. Find the link or go directly to https://adwords.google.com/select/main?cmd=KeywordSandbox. I don't mean good to imply this is enough for your success; the Google keyword suggestion tool will simply familiarize you with synonyms of your word and the approximate cost and search volume for that term.

Search volume does not translate into sales. For this reason, we offer eBay data mining research on Mauiceo.com, including keyword analysis. We are able to tell you which search terms associated with your product resulted in the highest actual sales. Wow! Use that data to be the core keywords you pay for on Google and Yahoo.

Finally, I **strongly** recommend a pilot here. Test out keywords to see which work best. Your pilot can test not only keywords, but the ads themselves. Remember our Helio example above? I noticed the cheap price in the second ad because it was in the title—and the third ad lost out because their (even lower) price was hidden in the body text.

When you do your pilot, Google will walk you through the process: identifying keywords, location (choose US only), and maximum spend per day. When you come to the Ad Serving selection, choose "Rotate" and not "Optimize." This will rotate your keywords equally and you can see which ones work best. Once the pilot is done and you're ready to start the campaign, you can go back to the Optimize default.

Yahoo Sponsored Search

Yahoo claims that they are the Web's most popular destination. This is quite a claim. Anyway, their version of Adwords is called Sponsored Search. Just click "Search Marketing" off the Yahoo home page or type www.searchmarketing.yahoo.com.

The steps are similar:

1. Identify keywords for your pilot; Yahoo also has a keyword research tool in their account management setup process.

2. Set your pilot to test different versions and "serve" each version equally; review your results

3. Identify your final marketing ad/keywords and set your maximum daily budget

4. Launch!

One cool, new feature that Yahoo has is a deal with PayPal. If you have a PayPal express checkout account (which you do, if you followed my steps in previous chapters), then your business ad—once displayed through Yahoo Sponsored Search—has a shopping cart next to the ad. This lets viewers know you have a safe checkout procedure on your site. I would prefer something different than a simple shopping cart, but hey, it does make you stand out in the search results—and that's what our efforts are all about! See the little shopping cart below?

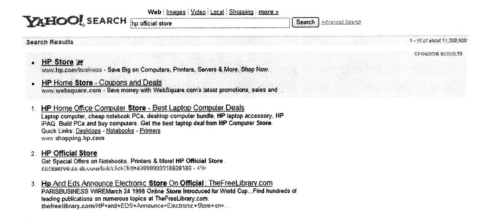

Google and Yahoo Promotions

Like everyone else on the web, Google and Yahoo are both trying to effectively promote small businesses. Specifically, both offer frequent "sign-up" credits for new advertisers. Here are a couple offers I found:

- Get $75 credit on Yahoo, see http://sponsoredsearch.yahoo.com/now, promo code US2127

- Get $100 credit on Yahoo AND free PayPal processing through Feb 28, 2008. Go to www.searchmarketing.yahoo.com/paypal.

Offers should be out there for you; just visit any of the popular coupon code sites (like www.promotioncodes.com) to search for the latest promotion.

A quick note on evaluating your pilot data: consumers are taking much longer to buy, and therefore you need to be mindful of this when calculating your paid search return[103]. According to a 2007 survey, "shoppers are taking on average 34 hours and 19 minutes from the time they first visit an ecommerce site to when they finally make a purchase."[104] This delay is in part because consumers are more cautious, but also because comparison shopping capability means buyers have more sources to choose from.

Paid Search on Shopping Comparison Sites

I mentioned early in the book how I often use www.mysimon.com when looking for a product I know I want to buy, because it will compare prices of the product across the web. I just enter my zip code, hit Go, and pick the low price provider, unless their feedback score raises a red flag. If so, I just go to the next low-cost provider. I couldn't confirm the source, but a company called channeladvisor[105] says that "80% of online purchases are influenced by comparison shopping."

Well, from a small business perspective, this is a hidden gem for us. We are the low-cost provider! You should investigate each of these sites and integrate your product offering on each site. Start out with:

- Mysimon
- PriceGrabber
- Shopping.com
- Shopzilla
- Nextag
- Google Product Search

---

103. This is counter to our 4-Hr work-week friend, who makes you draw conclusions from only a couple days' worth of data. See *The 4-Hour Workweek* (Crown Publishing, 2007), Timothy Ferriss pg. 173.
104. See http://www.marketwire.com/2.0/release.do?id=749599.
105. See www.channeladvisor.com

- Smarter.com
- Jellyfish

This is a great outsourcing task for elance.com. Let the winning bidder do all the work, and since your product is niched, your low price should stand out like a big candy cane. In this scenario, you could investigate the process for providing a higher price on the comparison sites—higher than your normal price, lower than the competitors.

Search Engine Optimization (SEO)

We move from paid search to search engine optimization. This is a holy grail of sorts—getting placed high in the results for free. In the early days of Google, we would sort through 3 or 4 pages of results without losing patience. Now, we hardly even scroll down the first screen—and if we do scroll, it is impatiently. Google and the other search engines have gotten better, over time, delivering results that are closer and closer to what you had in mind when you executed your search.

A couple years ago, the best way to get high placement involved 1) coming up with the right keywords at the hidden 'top' of your website, called "metatags;" and 2) "submitting" your site to each search engine so they knew about you. This involved about $100 and filling out a form; in a couple months, you would appear in that search engine's directory, similar to the online yellow pages.

Today, search engine optimization is a specialized task that is part art and part science. Don't waste your time doing it yourself; IF you figure out one part of the process, your success would be short-lived. For instance, Google had a major upgrade to their search algorithms (called "Florida") and businesses' sites who were ranking high, were now nowhere to be found. Getting high placement is a moving target. For instance, what is the key factor today for high placement (i.e. being "search engine optimized")?

Link traffic is currently the 800 pound gorilla in search engine optimization. Your website gets higher placement when multiple websites have permanent links to your site. The better those sites are (i.e. traffic), then your site gets pulled up, too. It's analogous to sports: the better the sports team (like Duke basketball), the higher rated is the academic institution (i.e. Duke's medical school). I would describe getting good links as a labor-intensive process. As a result, you can go out and "buy" links. I discourage this, because one, it's expensive, and two, Google and Yahoo are too smart and will detect this type of shenanigan. Buying links is a short-term solution.

Here's my basic recommendation: spend a little money and have someone do basic SEO for you, and spend the rest of your marketing dollars are CPC paid searches on Google and Yahoo.

On date of writing, I see eight "Guru Express" packages for search engine optimization that are $100 or less. There is one package with monthly updating for about $20 per month. I would select something like this to give your site basic search engine optimization. Then spend the good money as described above. When selecting the vendor, choose one that is not submitting your website through an automated tool; you want them to manually put your website in search engines and directories, do the meta tags & SEO copywriting, and create, validate, and submit XML sitemaps.

Let me say this a different way: unless you've got money, you can't win the battle of search engine optimization and being on page one all the time. So do the minimum level required and move on. What if you do have some extra marketing dollars?

ChannelAdvisor

If you do have some Marketing budget, consider using channeladvisor. They consolidate the two previous categories—paid search and SEO—for you.

For instance, instead of having your web-person manually connect with all the price comparison sites—channel advisor will do it for you. Their "comparison shopping" product will let you review all your campaigns on all sites in the same dashboard, and make a single change (like price or description) that is distributed to all comparison sites.

Similarly, their "search" product helps you automate and manage your paid search campaigns around search engines like Ask.com, MSN, Yahoo and Google.

Since channeladvisor has a business model that is small business friendly, and they understand how eBay fits into our model, I can recommend them. They don't charge license fees for their services or software, but rather take a cut on each successful sale.

In a way paid search is like math or finance: you should learn to do it manually first; once perfected, consider turning it over to the experts. If you want another option, consider www.marketing.networksolutions.com or www.webuildpages.com. Both are focused upon SEO and are highly stocked with Link Builders which help accomplish the task.

Getting the Word Out—Virally

YouTube was founded in February 2005, about the same time I finished writing the first edition of this book. Between then and now, YouTube has become one of the most important "Web 2.0" companies to date, eclipsed perhaps only by MySpace. The rise of YouTube has many implications, including one for *Maui CEO* businesses—viral marketing campaigns.

Viral marketing started, in my mind, when Hotmail started including branded signature lines on their free Hotmail account users. To wit, every email sent by Hotmail users was marketing Hotmail's free mail services. This is a good starting point for Viral marketing.

Today, businesses are starting to create videos that advertise their products or services. Using humor or some other way to make the video interesting. The video is posted and, it is hoped, downloaded and forwarded frequently enough to facilitate sales. It's difficult to know where the social phenomenon of viral videos will lead in the business space.

For instance, a viral video called "Cubicle War 2006" advertised for Windward, a software reporting company for developers. "Cubicle War 2006" has been viewed over a million times. Wow! When asked about whether they have sold product as a result of the viral video, their VP of Marketing noted the following: "Sales haven't increased dramatically since the video went live, and no one who's purchased the product has said that they did so because of the video. But over a million people have now heard of the company."[106]

There is, therefore, a great tension here: should you spend money developing a viral campaign when accurate conversion metrics are not even available (at time of writing)? Here are a few tips, which may seem obvious a year or two from now:

- Don't pretend that you're not advertising. The small time window for such has already passed. Everything is transparent now.

- Don't spend more than $10,000 on a viral video in any situation. I spent $600 on two viral videos (animated) on mauiceo.com—check them out.

- Successful viral videos seem to be irreverent, funny and/or weird. I'd take a clue from movie trailers that are available on Fandango: tell a story but leave them hanging. This "cliff-hanger" gets the watcher to go visit your site. Alternatively, you can have a coupon or promotion code at the end, which attempts to serve the same purpose

- Investigate advertising on the video-sharing sites. These free sites have to make money to stay in business, and users understand that.

---

106. http://www.webvideouniverse.com/marketing/article.php/3661841

Early users of Adwords (like me) had low cost-per-click fees and very strong ROI. Perhaps tomorrow's technology will allow granular connections between user profiles, search terms, and one-to-one marketing on sites like Revver and YouTube.

- Consider posting to the Tier II sites, where your chance of getting on the front page are much higher.

If you want to see a viral video that works, search for "iPhone Blendtec."

Conclusion

Today is August 20, 2007, and I am just finishing up my revisions to Maui CEO. How appropriate, then, that my final words come from Maui—literally! I am staring at some beautiful pink flamingos playing in the water and enjoying my people-watching at the Westin Maui.

As I close up the loose-ends, I received a great email from Mr. Hassan, a Canadian. Here's an excerpted summary from his email:

> Dear Mr. Tennant,
>
> What a clever and concise book! I have been thinking about an online business for a long time, and your book provided me the re-assurance that the idea is not so crazy after all.
>
> One thing I did not get from the book was whether selling goods around $20 in value could be successful. Also, is it true that only container loads are good for what you recommend?
>
> Best Wishes and Kind Regards,
>
> Sunny-Omer Hassan

Well, that's a great couple of questions as we conclude this journey together. Let me analogize to the Adkins diet. Dr. Adkins says that, in order for his diet to work, you can't do a low-fat version; you need to follow the steps, and by reducing the large majority of carbohydrates in your diet, your body will burn the fat. If you choose to pick and choose the parts of the diet to follow and not to follow, well, your results will be mixed.

In the context of Maui CEO, this is also true: you need to stick with the program because the parts are interrelated to each other. If you choose to sell items with selling prices around $20, as Mr. Hassan suggested above, you lose a key item: barrier to entry by competitors. Likewise, if you don't import by the container load (or least by LCL), then you have to pay wholesale price—just like everyone else. As we've mentioned over and over, selling on eBay—which reflects all of online commerce—is selling at wholesale. Buying at wholesale and selling at wholesale is not a recipe for small business success, especially given that search bots will put constant pressure on your margins and ability to compete against the bigger players.

There are short-term opportunities. To be balanced, here's an example where buying small lots from a wholesaler has decent margin—at least for now:

I found a great deal on 8x sport binoculars from an import consolidator called Global Sources Direct—$20.95 per unit if you buy a case of 10 units. Searching sales on eBay, which includes all brands of 8x binoculars like Carl Zeiss and Burris, the average price of sold units was $80.98. Pretty darn good! The numbers themselves look pretty solid across the board: binoculars had a sell-through percentage of 45%, with 29 pairs sold in 30 days. Using the return on capital invested in inventory (ROCII) idea from the latter part of Chapter 2, this is a reasonable proposition ... if you can sell a whole lot of binoculars. What's hidden in the sales data (and I can provide for you with data-mining services on the website) is this: there were only two sellers per day, on average. What does that tell you? Full-blown competition has not yet hit this niche. Companies like Global Sources Direct do the importing for you, and tend to keep out individual buyers by requiring bulk purchases. However, this is a short-term solution, because someone is at that manufacturer buying product by the container load—while you and every other supplier who buys from GSD—just paid more.

Unlike this short-term opportunity, I have given you a framework that will work for the medium-term. Thereafter, your own success is determined by you. Feel free to send questions or comments to info@mauiceo.com.

I wish you all the success in the world.

APPENDIX

For your reference and with hearty thanks to eBay, the following Appendix is a list of exhibitors at their 2007 Developer's Conference.

EXHIBITORS

Auction Video, Inc.

BOOTH 1030

www.auctionvideo.com

Join the millions worldwide who have found success with Auction Video technology. Show your buyers what you are selling and how your item works. It is fast, easy, and convenient. Visit Auction Video—and increase your sales today—the Auction Video way.

Auction123, Inc.

BOOTH 255

www.auction123.com

Auction123 is the premier solution for automotive Internet marketing and inventory management solutions. Our service line offers unparalleled Web-based management software, real-time inventory integration to a dealership's Web site with export to leading third-party classifieds, and superior nationwide full-service data collection and photography.

AuctionCheckout

BOOTH 455

www.AuctionCheckout.com

AuctionCheckout is a preferred payment technology for eBay sellers. It's never been easier to accept credit card payments for your auctions and for your Web site. Now buyers can click and make payments securely and quickly with no registration or enrollment required. It's fast, easy, and completely integrated with eBay. Check out online at www.auctioncheckout.com

AuctionSplash, Ltd.

BOOTH 1232

www.auctionsplash.com

AuctionSplash is a cool new utility that's brilliant for buying and selling on eBay. It runs on your desktop and brings, "Watch Lists", "Bids", and "Questions" automatically to you in the background. The Create Listing feature enables you to design sophisticated auctions with over 100 FREE templates and FREE picture hosting (including Supersize).

AuctionWagon

BOOTH 765

www.auctionwagon.com

Complete eBay consignment software for drop-off stores, franchises, postal stores, and individuals. AuctionWagon Store Manager G2 provides integrated consignor tracking, barcoding, shipping, consignor's Web site, check writing, photo editing, custom emails, POS, and more. Formerly an original eBay drop-off store, AuctionWagon has brought its real-world experience to G2's power and simplicity.

Auctionwire

BOOTH 450

www.auctionwireinc.com

Auctionwire is a full-service auction agency working with the world's largest corporations, foundations, ad agencies, and charities to create, manage, and run high-profile online auctions. Auctionwire specializes in fundraising, publicity, cause marketing, and asset recovery. Auctionwire operates addlivevoice.com and bidqualify.com providing value-added specialty services to its clients.

Auctiva

BOOTH 1032

www.auctiva.com

Auctiva's free eBay auction management tools substantially improve a seller's business. There are no hidden charges or fees. Auctiva customers enjoy free, unlimited image hosting with editing tools, unlimited templates, scheduling, stores, store windows, automatic feedback, 24/7 customer support, and more. Simply put, there is no better solution for eBay sellers.

auctomatic

Auctomatic

BOOTH 127

www.auctomatic.com

Auctomatic saves you time and money. It's the first a-la-carte PowerSeller solution that lets you choose exactly the features you want to pay for! No longer do you have to be burdened with features you don't need. Our focus is on simplicity and listening to what you want.

EXHIBITORS

 Avalara. Making sales tax less taxing.

Avalara, Inc.
BOOTH 1251
www.avalara.com

Make sales tax less taxing with Avalara for eBay ProStores! Achieve sales tax compliance, dramatically reduce audit exposure, and save time and money to focus on your real business. Eliminate your obsolete, error-prone ways of calculating, collecting, reporting on, and remitting sales taxes. Add Avalara sales tax automation to eBay ProStores now! Visit booth #1251 or www.avalara.com

 Avanquest*software*

Avanquest Software
BOOTH 1239
www.avanquestusa.com

Avanquest Software provides consumers and small businesses with award-winning software for PC maintenance, office productivity, communications, and mobility. Avanquest Software's presence in North America—consisting of Avanquest USA and Nova Development—offers a portfolio of more than 175 software titles available at 10,000 retail locations, on the Web, and through OEM partnerships. More information is available at www.avanquestusa.com and www.novadevelopment.com

Avery Dennison
BOOTH 117
www.avery.com

Avery Dennison Worldwide Office Products is a leading manufacturer of self-adhesive labels for laser and ink-jet printers, do-it-yourself business cards, T-shirt transfers, binders, dividers, and other office- and home-related supplies. For more information about Avery-brand products, please visit our Web site at www.avery.com or contact our Consumer Service Center at 1-800-GO-AVERY (1-800-462-8379).

Better Packages, Inc.
BOOTH 1228
www.betterpackages.com

Better Packages, Inc. products provide eBay users and businesses with efficient package sealing solutions that create secure, professional looking, tamper-evident packages. Our products help eBay sellers and buyers successfully "Seal the Deal". Stop by booth #1228, see how our products can help enhance your item listings and boost positive feedback!

BidPay
BOOTH 328
www.bidpay.com

BidPay, a CyberSource company, provides robust auction payment services that integrate directly into your online auctions. Take advantage of lower fees and accept Domestic & International credit cards without a need for a merchant account. Dedicated customer service, superior fraud management, and free Seller Protection make BidPay a better way to pay.

BizFilings
BOOTH 757
www.bizfilings.com

Protect your personal assets and gain tax advantages by incorporating your eBay Store. BizFilings professionally forms corporations and LLCs in all 50 states faster than anyone else. Our rush services make it possible to file in as little as 24 hours. No legal fees. Guaranteed. Get started today!

Business Plan Pro
BOOTH 951
www.paloaltosoftware.com

Palo Alto Software, an eBay Certified Solution Provider, produces the most recommended and best-selling business planning software available. Business Plan Pro® provides easy-to-use tools to help you run and grow a successful business on eBay. Get your business plan for eBay done quickly and efficiently with Business Plan Pro

EXHIBITORS

CASIO.

Casio, Inc.
BOOTH 217
www.casio.com

Casio—high-performance people, working together to bring innovative, personalized, digital products, and solutions to meet our customers' evolving lifestyles. Casio markets digital cameras, timepieces, calculators, keyboards, cash registers, and many other consumer electronic products. Visit us online at www.casio.com

channeladvisor

ChannelAdvisor Corporation
BOOTH 423
www.channeladvisor.com

ChannelAdvisor Corporation provides technology and services that enable industry-leading retailers and manufactures to sell their products across multiple online marketplaces such as eBay, Amazon.com, and Overstock.com, comparison shopping engines such as Shopping.com, Shopzilla, Nextag, and Froogle, and search engines such as Google, Yahoo!, and MSN. For more information, visit www.channeladvisor.com

CityMax
BOOTH 1241
www.citymax.com

Why settle for an average Web site when you can have one loaded with all the features usually only found on the big sites—for under $20! This includes catalog pages that integrate with eBay and PayPal payment processing. Do it all yourself, without any programming or design experience whatsoever. Come visit us for our special eBay Live! offer!

Cloud Dome, Inc.
BOOTH 460
www.clouddome.com

The Cloud Dome is a portable, affordable photography studio-in-a-bag. It's the simplest way for anyone to take professional-quality digital photographs without complicated lighting. Made of high impact, non-yellowing, crack-resistant plastic. Cloud Dome evenly diffuses natural light over the surface area of the object being shot.

Constant Contact
BOOTH 1029
www.constantcontact.com

Constant Contact is the leading email marketing service for small businesses, associations, and non-profits. With more than 100,000 customers today, Constant Contact helps small businesses and organizations succeed in building lasting customer relationships through professional email communications, including newsletters, announcements, promotions, and more. To learn more, visit www.constantcontact.com or call (781) 472-8100.

Cutting Edge Packaging Products
BOOTH 138
www.4bubble.com

Cutting Edge Packaging Products is a wholesale supplier of packaging and shipping supplies including bubble mailers, bubble wrap, packing tape, boxes, and more. Our price, quality, and service can't be beat. Visit us on the Web at www.4bubble.com or call toll free: 888-720-3343 ext. 7. eBay User ID: cuttingedgepackaging

Dependable Auto Shippers, Inc.
BOOTH 146
www.dasautoshippers.com

Dependable Auto Shippers, Inc. provides vehicle relocation services for individuals, corporate relocation professionals, and many others. Moving over 100,000 vehicles each year, DAS has been setting the industry standards for over 50 years as the leader in vehicle relocation services.

DIRECTCAPITAL®

Direct Capital Corp.
BOOTH 1054
http://financing-center.ebay.com/ebaybusiness

Buyers need cost-effective solutions for purchasing large-ticket business items on eBay, and you can answer their call by offering financing. Equipment Financing for eBay, provided by Direct Capital Corp., will help you increase sales, get paid fast, eliminate non-paying bidders, and get your Final Value Fees reimbursed! Sign up today!

EXHIBITORS

Doba
BOOTH 417
www.doba.com

Doba's Product Sourcing Platform simplifies product sourcing for Internet retailers. Providing a simple way to find and sell products online, Doba connects retail merchants to a virtual warehouse of wholesale products, which can be drop-shipped directly to the buyer.

DYMO Corporation
BOOTH 229
www.dymo.com/postage

DYMO is a recognized leader in innovative solutions that help people organize their world. DYMO offers a complete range of labeling products, accessories, and postage solutions. DYMO Stamps™ no-monthly fee solution is the fast and easy way to print USPS®-approved labels. DYMO LabelWriters® and labels have also been integrated into eBay's online postage application.

eAuction Depot
BOOTH 432
www.eauction-depot.com

Open an eAuction Depot eBay drop-off store and service people in your neighborhood who have more than $2,000 of unused valuables. Our turnkey franchise costs under $80,000 and includes software for 15 years, a 200 item store system, training, complete site selection, and much more.
1-866-651-6424 or www.eauction-depot.com

eBay™ Mastercard®
BOOTH 1023
www.mastercard.ebay.com

Introducing the new eBay Mastercard—the card that rewards you for every purchase: no matter where you shop. It's the safe way to pay because you're protected against fraud or items not received and includes 24x7 customer support. Plus, redeem your points toward future eBay purchases and even your seller fees

eBay Radio
BOOTH 865
www.wsRadio.com/eBayRadio

eBay Radio is hosted by Jim "Griff" Griffith, Dean of eBay Education. The show broadcasts live every Tuesday from 11am–2pm PST with expert guests and call ins. "The Sunday Ask Griff Show" is from 3pm–5pm PST and is strictly call ins. All shows are archived for 24/7 listening on demand, podcasts are also available. Produced by wsRadio.com, listen at www.wsRadio.com/eBayRadio

Endicia
BOOTH 1017
www.endicia.com

Take advantage of substantially lower shipping rates and avoid hidden charges by integrating the USPS into your fulfillment mix. Endicia's solutions include standalone desktop shipping tools, database integration, Web services, customizable APIs, and integration into over 60 third party applications. Try it free for 30 days at www.endicia.com

eSupplyStore.com
BOOTH 317
www.eSupplyStore.com

eSupplyStore.com is an eBay Platinum PowerSeller of high-quality, low-priced shipping and packaging supplies. Items offered include bubble mailers, bubble wrap, tape, boxes, packing peanuts, and much, much more. Look for the seller eSupplyStore on eBay, or visit www.esupplystore.com for the lowest prices and fastest shipping on all of your packaging supply needs.

EXHIBITORS

Everest Software, Inc.
BOOTH 561
www.everestsoftwareinc.com

Everest Software empowers companies to view and manage every function of their business. Our fully-integrated business management software, Everest, addresses every need of SMBs in the wholesale/distribution and retail industries by allowing them to manage and track their business operations online and offline-- from storefront to the back-office.

FileMaker, Inc.
BOOTH 856
www.filemaker.com

FileMaker Pro is the #1-selling easy-to-use database for Windows and Mac OS. Come by booth 856 to learn how FileMaker Pro can help you spend less time managing information and more time on what's important to the success of your business. FileMaker, Inc. is a subsidiary of Apple, Inc.

FillZ
BOOTH 1035
www.fillz.com

FillZ is your one-stop Inventory, Re-pricing, and Order Management Solution. Load inventory once and list on up to 14 marketplaces including eBay, Amazon, and more. Manage your inventory through FillZ Web-based interface or integrate with your own application via FillZ FTP site. Try it free for 30 Days.

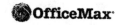

EXHIBITORS

FP International
BOOTH 656
www.fpintl.com

FP International, with 40 years experience in industrial packaging, is introducing the MINI PAK'R, a "tabletop" air cushion machine designed for small businesses and individual shippers.

The MINI PAK'R makes six different cushions, including bubble. It's easy to use, works for most packing needs while eliminating bulky rolls and bags of packaging.

Freightquote.com
BOOTH 1234
www.freightquote.com

Freightquote.com is the leading online marketplace for freight transportation and the solution behind the eBay freight Shipping Calculator utility. Sellers easily incorporate the calculator from the Sell Your Item function. Freightquote.com gives eBay customers great carriers, great rates, and great customer service. It's fast, easy, and free to use.

GENCO Marketplace
BOOTH 1229
www.gencomarketplace.com

GENCO Marketplace is the premier liquidator of returned and excess merchandise. For buyers, we provide a large, steady supply of product, an easy online purchasing process, and a low-risk trading environment. For sellers, we provide access to a global buyer network and tools to maximize recovery value. For more information, visit www.gencomarketplace.com

global sources

Global Sources Direct
BOOTH 1131
www.globalsourcesdirect.com

Global Sources Direct provides services enabling China's suppliers to sell products to eBay buyers. Global Sources is a leading business-to-business media company that facilitates global trade, with a particular focus on the China market, by providing information to international buyers and integrated marketing services to suppliers.

Gordon Brothers Group, LLC
BOOTH 339
www.gordonbrothers.com

With 23 buying offices located around the world, Gordon Brothers Wholesale is a unique source of better-branded clothing, accessories, home goods, giftware, and other consumer products.

Campaigner®
by GOT Corporation

GOT Corporation
BOOTH 351
www.campaigner.com

GOT Corporation's Campaigner products enable highly personalized one-to-one email dialogues. The Campaigner on-demand platform enables marketers to communicate with customers, measure their responses, and analyze those responses to interact in a more intelligent, automated way—resulting in more profitable relationships.

Government Liquidation
BOOTH 228
www.govliquidation.com

Government Liquidation in partnership with the U.S. Department of Defense holds an exclusive contract to sell Government Surplus Property to the public. Located nationwide, it's the ideal place to find items in over 600 categories to resell on eBay including trucks, scrap metal, collectibles, medical equipment, field gear, and cameras.

goWholesale
BOOTH 429
www.goWholesale.com

goWholesale is the leading wholesale search engine on the Internet, connecting eBay sellers, e-tailers, and retailers with hundreds of wholesale product sources, as well as services and information for starting and managing a business.

EXHIBITORS

HammerTap
BOOTH 933
www.hammertap.com

With HammerTap market research, you can remove all the guesswork to increase your sales and maximize your profits. Find out what sells and how to sell it, including the best ending day and listing duration, starting price, title keywords, and much more. Get HammerTap and get the Power to Profit!

iGuru©
BOOTH 1255
www.igurulabs.com

iGuru is the world's first real-life software publisher. iGuru integrates your work & personal life-style. It democratizes software amply: affordability; multi-OS compatibility; true single interface vs. Suites; Modularity as diverse as you. AuctionGuru™ is the new breakthrough, full-cycle eBay solution...Release your inner joy, power.

Imprintor
BOOTH 1129
www.imprintor.com

Tap into your share of a multi-billion dollar industry by starting your own business or complementing your current company! Customize promotional products with the economical Imprintor Pad Printing System! Ideal for small quantity printing, product sampling, and business promotions. Get professional quality imprints on plastics, ceramics, glass, and flexible foams.

Infopia
BOOTH 917
www.infopia.com

Infopia provides an award-winning eCommerce management platform that enables online retailers to grow and optimize their business. Sell on multiple channels, manage inventory, fulfillment, and customer relationships, plus, analyze performance—all from a single platform. Infopia offers a scalable solution to easily automate business processes and integrate with other solutions.

Interapptive ShipWorks
BOOTH 554
www.interapptive.com

Interapptive ShipWorks helps sellers manage and ship orders. ShipWorks automates tasks and helps improve customer service. Copying and pasting is eliminated with direct downloads from eBay, ChannelAdvisor, CRE Loaded, Infopia, Marketworks, Miva Merchant, osCommerce, ProStores, ShopSite, and Yahoo! Stores. ShipWorks includes integrated support for FedEx, UPS, USPS, Stamps.com, and Endicia.

iwascoding
BOOTH 234
www.iwascoding.com

iwascoding develops Mac software since 1995. One of its hottest products is GarageSale, an eBay listing utility. GarageSale integrates tightly with Apple's operating system and creates an unparalleled eBay experience for the Mac OS X user.

Jackson Hewitt Tax Service, Inc.
BOOTH 428
www.jacksonhewitt.com

Jackson Hewitt Tax Service®, with over 6,500 offices throughout the United States during the 2007 tax season, is an industry leader providing full service individual federal and state income tax preparation. Most offices are independently owned and operated. The company is based in Parsippany, NJ. Visit www.jacksonhewitt.com to learn more.

Kompolt
BOOTH 354
www.kompolt.com

The original online auction agency, Kompolt (www.kompolt.com) is a marketing agency that concentrates on promoting brands and building brand trust through high-profile, high-value charity auctions. Non-profits, agencies, and top brands turn to Kompolt to design, create, and manage the eCommerce segments of their Cause Marketing and other promotional campaigns.

EXHIBITORS

Kyozou
BOOTH 439
www.kyozou.com

All elements of online commerce are seamlessly brought together by fully integrating multi-channel selling, search marketing, shopping cart management, Web and auction templates, bar-coded inventory, location/franchise management, automated shipping, and many more automation tools and services. Kyozou ties together all elements of online commerce in one easy-to-use application.

LaunchPad Auctions
BOOTH 341
www.launchpadauctions.com

LaunchPadAuctions.com creates custom-designed Auction Templates, eBay Stores, Flash Animation, About Me, Custom Pages, and Web sites. Please check out our portfolio. We will create a strong cross-promotion campaign to help increase your eBay and or Web site sales. We also offer strategy and marketing consulting and training.

Lift Mates, Inc.
BOOTH 860
www.liftmates.com

The Lift Mates Solo Lift is an innovative tool that allows you to safely and easily lift boxes with only one hand! Use your free hand to open doors, climb stairs, and more. It also reduces the stress and strain on your spine. We've got your back!

Liquidation.com
BOOTH 433
www.liquidation.com

Liquidation.com has the hottest products ready for you to resell on eBay. Find overstock electronics, apparel, computers, tools, toys, and much more! Products are sold in bulk lots via online auction and start at just $100! Visit Liquidation.com today and find out why we're a #1 source for eBay PowerSellers!

List'd Express
BOOTH 1028
www.listd.com

Fast, easy, and free eBay listing tool for sellers with any level of experience! The easiest and most user-friendly eBay sellers tool on the market. A one-page listing tool that would help you get an item up for sale in just minutes.

ListQueue Software
BOOTH 663
www.listqueue.com

eBay's first end-to-end auction management solution designed and created by professional eBay sellers & Trading Assistants. ListQueue has the features, functionality, and ease of use you requested while still fully integrating powerful tools to manage your business on eBay. Manage your consigners, inventory, listings, photos, payments, and statements with ListQueue.

Litestage Lighting Systems
BOOTH 438
www.litestage.com

Litestage is a complete, self-contained, do-it-yourself product photography lighting system. Litestage eliminates shadows, hot spots and reflections providing consistent and controlled lighting. With Litestage you can easily create professional quality images for Web sites, catalogs and auctions. Comes with integrated strobe (flash) and tungsten lamps. 30"x30"x24" inside.

MarketBlast
BOOTH 929
www.marketblast.com

MarketBlast is your eBay Control Panel—helping you manage all aspects of your growing business on eBay. From inventory tracking to creating listings, from customer relationship management to PayPal and Endicia integration, MarketBlast is packed with everything you need to be an eBay PowerSeller, all with no monthly fees.

EXHIBITORS

Marketworks
BOOTH 823
www.marketworks.com

Thousands of traditional and online businesses depend on Marketworks to power their eCommerce operations to target millions of shoppers. Marketworks is the leading solution for hosting and managing Web store sales, eBay and Amazon sales, shopping comparison sites, and search engine marketing programs all from a single platform. Visit www.marketworks.com

MerchantAdvantage
BOOTH 1245
www.merchantadvantage.com

MerchantAdvantage introduces Channel Management with Chanalytics for ProStores and eBay Stores clients. Feed and optimize your product catalog to over 90 marketing channels with a few, simple clicks. Then, analyze these marketing campaigns and react to them immediately. Expand marketing efforts intelligently with the only tool-based, channel marketing solution in the marketplace with analytics. Booth 1245, across from the PayPal Pavilion.

MerchantRun
BOOTH 563
www.merchantrun.com

Why limit yourself to a single eBay market? Take your business global! MerchantRun is the leading provider of eBay cross-border trade solutions. Only MerchantRun allows you to manage your sales on more than 20 eBay sites using one convenient interface. Expand your markets and your sales with MerchantRun!

Microsoft Corporation
BOOTH 945
www.microsoft.com

Microsoft Office Accounting Express 2007 gives you the tools you need to reach out to millions of eBay customers. Easily list your products, track activity, and process sales orders. Available integration with PayPal means you get paid faster. Visit Microsoft booth #945 and get your FREE CD.

Monster
BOOTH 223
www.monster.com

Monster has everything eBay sellers need to grow their small businesses--from online hiring tools to expert advice on how to interview and hire top candidates. Whether you want to post a job or search resumes, Monster is the easy, cost-effective way to find the help you need fast.

MyLLC.com
BOOTH 135
www.MyLLC.com

MyLLC.com offers customers complete entity formation, entity dissolutions, certificates of good standing, amendments, trademark searches and registrations, registered agent services, corporate services, and corporate supplies such as corporate kits, stock certificates, and embossing seals. Mention coupon code ebay69 to incorporate or form an LLC for only $69 (plus state & shipping fees).

NFIB
The Voice of Small Business®.

National Federation of Independent Business
BOOTH 1247
www.nfib.com

The National Federation of Independent Business is America's most powerful small-business advocacy group. A nonprofit, non-partisan organization, NFIB fights for the right to own, operate, and grow your business. We represent our members' interests on the state and national level, and offer products and services tailored to saving small businesses time and money.

Office of the State Treasurer and Receiver General of Massachusetts
BOOTH 1253
www.mass.gov/treasury

Office of the State Treasurer and Receiver General of Massachusetts Treasurer Timothy P. Cahill manages over $100 billion in the Treasury's departments including the Abandoned Property Division, which has paid over $158 million in claims in the last four years and holds eBay auctions of unclaimed property from safe deposit boxes.

EXHIBITORS

Ontronics
BOOTH 953
www.ontronics.com

Ontronics™ is a Texas-based, global services company focused on enabling select segments of the wireless industry through specialized supply chain programs. We specialize in New, Used, Carrier Return, and Refurbished CDMA & GSM Mobile Phones. A few of the models which we currently have in stock are: Motorola V3 GSM, K1, V3C CDMA, V3M, E815, V551, V330 LG VX8100, VX8500, VX6100, and VX5200.

Ortery Technologies, Inc.
BOOTH 350
www.ortery.com

Start taking better pictures today! Ortery manufactures PC-Controlled photography studios (Photosimile) and photo automation tools anyone can use to create shadow-free, professional images (in seconds) for use on eBay and Web sites. Photosimile software contains specifically designed features to assist in taking and publishing pictures for eBay.

Pak Mail Centers of America, Inc.
BOOTH 925
www.pakmail.com

Pak Mail is the world's premier packing and shipping solutions center. From priceless and sentimental to oversize and overweight, we pack and ship single pieces, warehouse inventories, and freight for the eBay Community. Services: domestic/international shipping by air, ground, ocean, bulk, recurring, large freight and special handling, custom packing/crating, pick up, delivery.

PARATURE.

Parature
BOOTH 332
www.parature.com

Parature, the market leader in on-demand customer support software solutions, enables organizations to improve their internal and external support systems while reducing costs. The company's flagship product is an easy-to-use, comprehensive, and affordable customer service solution for associations, businesses, educational institutions, and government agencies. Parature enables organizations to manage all of their support needs through a fully integrated multi-channel solution. For more information please visit www.parature.com or call 1-877-GO-PARATURE.

Pearson Education
BOOTH 864
www.pearsoned.com

Pearson Education is the global leader in educational and professional publishing, providing scientifically research-based print and digital programs to help people of all ages learn at their own pace, in their own way. The company is home to such renowned publishing brands as IBM Press, Prentice Hall Professional, Addison-Wesley Professional, Peachpit Press, Cisco Press, Que Publishing, and InformIT.

Premier Products International
BOOTH 1058
www.ezdropship.com

Premier Products Int'l is a pioneer in the online dropship industry since 1998. We offer our customers the ability to order name brand products online to be shipped from our warehouse to their buyers. By utilizing EZDropship.com our customers are able to easily resell our products on eBay or create their own Web site pre-stocked with merchandise. We give you everything you need to start your business in one complete EZ system.

ProfitBuilderSoftware.com
BOOTH 1230
www.profitbuildersoftware.com

"Putting eBay fees back in your pocket"—That's our motto at ProfitBuilderSoftware.com. We have developed a patent-pending online software tool that allows eBay sellers to identify the best listing and pricing strategies to maximize profits.

EXHIBITORS

Prosper

BOOTH 1122

www.prosper.com

Prosper, America's first people-to-people lending marketplace, makes consumer lending more financially and socially rewarding for everyone. eBay users understand Prosper intuitively. Instead of listing and bidding on items, people list and bid on loans up to $25K using Prosper's auction platform. Visit booth 1122 for a t-shirt and a demonstration!

RedRoller

BOOTH 322

www.redroller.com

RedRoller provides eBay sellers with a free, one-stop shipping solution that compares prices and delivery options from major carriers. RedRoller makes shipping easier and faster with features like address verification, email notification, label printing, reporting, and full eBay integration. Schedule and track your shipping transactions in a few clicks.

Refund Retriever

BOOTH 134

www.refund-retriever.com

Your package arrives late, we get your shipping costs back. Refund Retriever is a shipment auditing company that helps UPS, FedEx, and DHL customers ensure all delivery guarantees are met, monitors for gross over-charges on your account by the shipping companies, and alerts you whenever shipment fraud is suspected.

RingCentral, Inc.

BOOTH 557

www.ringcentral.com

RingCentral provides online merchants with professional phone, fax, and voicemail services at a low price. Our award-winning technology is loaded with business features and works with any phone or computer in the world. There are no up-front costs and no hardware to buy. Pricing plans begin at $9.99 a month.

SAGEFIRE™

SageFire

BOOTH 833

www.sagefire.com

SageFire provides two essential tools for your growing success on eBay: YES!—the Year End Summary for all eBay activities by User ID by year (exclusively offered by SageFire) and KeepMore.net—accounting made simple with direct import of eBay bought and sold items. Visit Booth 833 to win a Lava Lamp!

Seamless Development

BOOTH 1133

www.seamlessdevelopment.com

Seamless Development was founded on the premise that state-of-the-art technological tools should be made available to everyone at an affordable cost. So whether you're a small business working hard to get ahead, a big business looking to improve efficiency, or launching the next great idea, Seamless Development offers the eServices to take you from concept to operation.

SHARPICS™
Digital Photography Solutions

Sharpics, Inc.

BOOTH 435

www.sharpics.com

Sharpics, Inc. is a trusted source in product photography with a complete line of cost-effective and innovative solutions for achieving professional product images. Innovators of D-Flector™ photo studio & backgrounds, tabletop monopod, compact studio lighting, and other photo studio accessories.

SquareTrade, Inc.

BOOTH 358

www.squaretrade.com

SquareTrade is the leading provider of online shopping services addressing the "trust deficit" in eCommerce. Established in 1999, SquareTrade delivers both pioneering and now industry-leading merchant verification, the SquareTrade Seller Seal program, extended warranty services, and online dispute resolution.

EXHIBITORS

Squidoo.com
BOOTH 1132
www.squidoo.com/ebayonsquidoo

Squidoo.com and eBay PowerSellers go together like chocolate and peanut butter: great apart, even better together. Find out how Squidoo can help drive more people to your auctions, tell better stories about your items for sale, and earn a bounty for you or for charity.

Surplus Sourcing Group, Inc.
BOOTH 1033
www.surplussourcing.com

Surplus Sourcing Group is a global leader in closeout and excess inventories of home electronics & computer related products with emphasis on profit margins for eCommerce sellers. We deal in digital camera, cordless phones, mobile phone, storage media, MP3 players, and more! As the exclusive Factory Refurbisher of Vivitar Digital Cameras and Vtech Cordless Phones, we offer great values to online sellers. We ship globally and do drop-shipping. Among the brands we offer: Vivitar, Vtech, Kodak, Logitech, Sandisk, 3com, Mustek, Agfa, Philips, Lexmark, Sampo, Ricoh, Lexar, IBM, HP, Creative, Viewsonic, Labtec, and others.

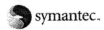

Symantec Corporation
BOOTH 1231
www.symantec.com

Symantec offers small businesses and consumers the most comprehensive Windows Protection solutions in the marketplace, to provide you and your customers confidence in a connected world. Whether you are transacting with a customer online, or making sure your electronic records are safe and secure, Symantec delivers easy to use and affordable products that will keep your business up and running.

TaxLoopholes
BOOTH 928
www.taxloopholes.com

TaxLoopholes™ is an education-based company that leads the industry in research and development of innovative tax strategies that allow individuals to proactively manage their tax planning. This strategic tax planning ultimately minimizes your tax liability while simultaneously maximizing your legal protection. Our goal at TaxLoopholes is to educate individuals and corporations on how to keep more of what they make.

Terapeak
BOOTH 532
www.terapeak.com

Terapeak's online research tool enables users to review closed eBay listings to determine future sales strategies. Sellers can assess average pricing, determine effective listing strategies, review trends, research competition, create sales reports, and keep an eye on hot sellers. eBay Certified Provider Terapeak provides a wealth of information in an easily accessible format.

The Occasions Group
BOOTH 454
www.theoccasionsgroup.com

For just $9.95, you can expand your business on eBay! Get thousands of products from invitations for weddings and parties to engraved giftware, favors, holiday cards, scrapbooking products and more. The CD has everything you need to start selling and we drop ship, so there is no inventory!

The Queen of Auctions
BOOTH 528
www.thequeenofauctions.com

Make all the money you deserve—quickly and easily! Boot Camp in a Box teaches you how, with the Dralle Method. Pre-order Lynn's *3rd 100 Best Things I've Sold on eBay* book, sign up for her free weekly eZine—and meet The Queen of Auctions, Lynn Dralle!

EXHIBITORS

TRUSTe
BOOTH 932
www.TRUSTe.com

TRUSTe helps consumers and businesses identify trustworthy online organizations through its Web Privacy Seal, Email Privacy Seal, and Trusted Download Programs. An independent, non-profit organization celebrating its 10th anniversary in 2007, TRUSTe certifies Web sites and resolves thousands of consumer privacy problems every year.

U-PIC Insurance Services
BOOTH 1017
www.u-pic.com

U-PIC Insurance Services provides discounted parcel insurance coverage for packages shipped via the U.S. Postal Service, UPS, FedEx, DHL, and LTL carriers. With 18 years of experience, U-PIC offers the highest level of risk management at a low cost. Contact U-PIC at 800-955-4623 Ext. 6306 or www.u-pic.com

U.S. Small Business Administration
BOOTH 552
www.sba.gov

The SBA's programs and services can assist you in almost every aspect of starting your business, from developing a business plan to obtaining financing, and from marketing your products and services to managing your company. Visit us at www.sba.gov

U.S. Small Business Transportation
BOOTH 955
www.freight101.com

Small Business Transportation/www.freight101.com is a third-party logistics company providing shipping services across the entire United States. Our user-friendly Web site gives you the ability to receive real-time quotes from hundreds of reputable carriers, at competitive prices. We've made the shipping process easy and cost-effective. Our rates, service, and technology have kept customers coming back for over 10 years.

uShip, Inc.
BOOTH 333
www.uShip.com

uShip is the largest online marketplace for shipping and moving services. Like eBay, which matches buyers and sellers, uShip connects people having shipping needs with feedback-rated transportation service providers. uShip's reverse-auction style marketplace means you always have the power to choose the best provider at the best price.

Vendio
BOOTH 817
www.Vendio.com

Vendio's services help eBay merchants reduce expensive marketplace fees by automating nearly every element of the sales process, including creating and editing items in bulk, publishing attractive product descriptions and images to eBay, keeping control of inventory, fulfilling orders, and merchandising more effectively to boost sales.

SELF-SERVICE DIRECT MARKETING

VerticalResponse®
BOOTH 1128
www.verticalresponse.com

VerticalResponse empowers small businesses to create, manage, and analyze their own email marketing campaigns in minutes, no matter what their level of technical expertise is!

VerticalResponse provides pre-designed email layouts, sending options, and superb email deliverability. At about 1¢ per email, it's the most affordable solution to help your business grow.

Vertus
BOOTH 359
www.vertustech.com

Fluid Mask is an Adobe Photoshop® plug-in tool based on breakthrough segmentation technology inspired by the way the eye, optic nerve, and brain perform visual processing. Fluid Mask's powerful segmentation engine analyzes the distribution of colors, gradients and textures within the image and finds the edges for you.

EXHIBITORS

Via Trading Corporation
BOOTH 329
www.viatrading.com

Via Trading specializes in dealing with Overstock, Customer Return, and Liquidation Merchandise. Based in Los Angeles, CA—Via Trading is a major wholesale drop shipper as well as a primary provider of goods to the secondary market such as eBay users, Online Vendors, Discount Stores, Flea Market/Swap Meet vendors, etc.

VisNetic Mailflow
BOOTH 352
www.visneticmailflow.com

VisNetic MailFlow is powerful, affordable email management and tracking software that automatically routes inbound email to the appropriate groups or individuals. It gives eBay sellers the tools necessary to answer emails quickly with knowledgeable, accurate responses, and it allows management to monitor email distribu-

tion and response times.

VistaPrint
BOOTH 126
www.vistaprint.com

With more than 8,000,000 customers worldwide, VistaPrint is the source for high-quality graphic design, Internet printing and premium service. We offer small businesses and consumers a convenient, high-quality solution for graphic design services and full-color printing in small quantities, without the premium price.

Index

978-0-595-34032-3
0-595-34032-6

Printed in the United States
105133LV00004B/286-288/A